ZEN
AND THE
ART
OF
RUNNING

ZEN
AND THE
ART
OF
RUNNING

THE PATH TO MAKING
PEACE WITH YOUR PACE

LARRY SHAPIRO, PhD

▲adamsmedia
Avon, Massachusetts

Published by
Adams Media, a division of F+W Media, Inc.
57 Littlefield Street, Avon, MA 02322. U.S.A.
www.adamsmedia.com

ISBN-10: 1-59869-960-1
ISBN-13: 978-1-59869-960-9

Printed in the United States of America.

J I H G F E D

Library of Congress Cataloging-in-Publication Data
is available from the publisher.

Readers are urged to take all appropriate precautions when undertaking any physical task. Always consult a physician before beginning any exercise program. Although every effort has been made to provide the best possible information in this book, neither the publisher nor the author are responsible for accidents, injuries, or damage incurred as the result of tasks undertaken by readers.

This publication is designed to provide accurate and authoritative information with regard to the subject matter covered. It is sold with the understanding that the publisher is not engaged in rendering legal, accounting, or other professional advice. If legal advice or other expert assistance is required, the services of a competent professional person should be sought.

—From a *Declaration of Principles* jointly adopted by a Committee of the American Bar Association and a Committee of Publishers and Associations

Many of the designations used by manufacturers and sellers to distinguish their product are claimed as trademarks. Where those designations appear in this book and Adams Media was aware of a trademark claim, the designations have been printed with initial capital letters.

This book is available at quantity discounts for bulk purchases.
For information, please call 1-800-289-0963.

CONTENTS

DEDICATION

*To my wife, Athena, and my daughters,
Thalia and Sophia, who don't really understand
but are willing to play along.*

ACKNOWLEDGMENTS

I owe a large debt to Steve Nadler, who helped "train me up" when I first landed in Madison, Wisconsin, and who introduced me to the best group of running companions for which one could hope. I wouldn't trade those pre-dawn Thursday morning runs with Steve, Pete, Jim, Wade, and Greg for anything. Thanks also to Dean, Katy, and Bill for joining along on those long training runs. And of course I can't forget (try as I might!) wisecracking Marc and Mike. I'm grateful to Mike in Sydney, Australia, for his companionship on many splendid runs in the Mosman area. Special thanks to Dean, who put me in touch with his daughter Katrina, who suggested this project to me. Thanks to Wendy, Renee, Casey, and Ashley at Adams Media. My wife, Athena, has been an invaluable editor and advisor in the course of writing this book. Finally, I'm very grateful to Jim Anderson, whose enthusiasm for Buddhism and confidence in me were inspirational.

INTRODUCTION

The stars lose their twinkle as the rising sun throws its own light into the sky. The night's silence gives way to a lone bird chirping, and soon other birds join in. The steady rhythm of your feet against pavement adds percussion to their song. A choral greeting welcomes the new day. You are moving through nature. You are part of nature, and nature is part of you. Do you recognize these moments? They are everywhere, all the time. This book will teach you how to find them through the activity of running. Whether you are a seasoned runner interested in enhancing your running experience, a novice curious about how to take your running to the next level, or a non-runner who has been searching for one more reason to give running a try, Zen has gifts to offer you.

Of course, there are lots of books available to runners or potential runners. Some of those books focus on getting results. They contain charts that specify how far and fast you must run over a four-month period if you want to cross the finish line below a certain time in a particular race. Other books concentrate on physical aspects of running. These offer advice about stride length, posture, arm swing, and other details that might interest runners who want to make their bodies perform more efficiently. This book will discuss some of those issues, but its main aim is not on results or on what you must do to optimize your running form. Rather, this book is about how to train your mind so you can maximize the pleasure you receive from running. There is a world out there, a beautiful world, and Zen will teach you how to run *with* it rather than *through* it.

The mental training you'll learn derives from various Zen Buddhist principles. There are many approaches to developing mental discipline, but Zen is unique in a number of respects. For one thing, Zen is a joyful philosophy. The goal of Zen is to reduce the anxieties, worries, and fears that often make people step through life apprehensively. For another, a Zen perspective seems especially well-suited to address the particular concerns that runners face. You'll discover what it is like to *run in the moment*, to feel acutely *aware* of the world around you.

Why is Zen good for runners? Most problems runners face are not physical, but mental. And most of these problems stem from misconceptions that Zen can help dispel. As you learn how to add a Zen dimension to your running, you'll come to understand concepts like *mindfulness, right effort, meditation, The Middle Way*, and *impermanence*. An appreciation of these ideas will help you cope with a number of obstacles that runners at all levels of experience sometimes face. So, this book is for any runner who:

Suffers from occasional motivational problems.
Do you sometimes have trouble getting out of bed and into your running shoes on those ice-cold, dark mornings? Do

you come home from work and just don't feel like running? The Zen practice of mindfulness can help you overcome these feelings.

Has a hard time juggling a running schedule with a family schedule.

Does your spouse or partner groan when you start to pull the laces on your shoes? Do your children remember who you are? Lots of runners feel guilty about taking valuable time away from their families. This is a complex issue, but a Zen perspective can help guide you toward a successful resolution.

Has difficulty enjoying available running routes.

Do you struggle to enjoy your running locale? Not all of us have the luxury of stepping out the door and finding ourselves in a runner's paradise. Learning how to enjoy running in busy cities, hot deserts, polar landscapes, and *terra incognita* requires skill. Zen concepts like mindfulness and right effort can help.

Is looking for greater fulfillment from running.

Do you still feel tense after a run? Zen Buddhism's focus on meditation as a source of tranquility and awareness makes it possible to draw unique pleasures from running. Running, it turns out, provides an excellent opportunity for practicing meditation techniques, which in turn promise to enhance your running experience.

Is seeking a training program that "fits."

Do you want to discover the best practice for *you*? The Zen idea of the Middle Way is crucial to a successful training program.

Zen teaches that extremes are harmful. There are methods to identify which is The Middle Way for you, and I will explain them in this book.

Wants to experience the pleasures of racing.

Are you interested in racing? Racing is often most successful when you are able to "disengage" your mind from your body. If you can distract your mind from the struggles your body faces as you race, you'll have an easier time of it and your performance will improve. Zen teaches how to narrow your concentration, so that you can endure races that might otherwise be beyond your ability.

Has been slowed by injuries or aging.

Do you struggle with injuries or advancing age? Runners make terrible patients. They tend not to allow themselves adequate time to heal, and many are unable to acknowledge that an injury or advancing age prevents them from running their former speeds and distances. A Zen point of view sheds a very different light on these issues, and makes the consequences of injury and aging easier to accept.

Of course, Zen is not only a philosophy for runners. It just so happens that running is the kind of activity that benefits tremendously when you apply Zen ideology. By the end of this book, you should be in a position to extend the lessons you have learned about running to the much more challenging activity of living.

I promise we'll have fun as we embark on this path. You'll hear about problems that are familiar to you, and testimonials from other runners will likely ring a bell. I think you'll enjoy trying out some of the solutions that a Zen perspective suggests, and you'll be surprised by the timelessness of the Buddha's advice. If you have spent any time running, you'll see a lot of yourself in this book. With commitment and practice, the pleasures Zen has brought to my running will become yours to embrace as well.

CHAPTER 1
ZEN MOTIVATION: GETTING OUT THE DOOR

How often does something come along that threatens to derail your running plans? Maybe the run has been on your calendar for weeks. It's that last twenty-mile training run before the marathon, or the annual benefit run that you've participated in for the past eight years. Maybe the run is nothing out of the ordinary—just your regular Thursday morning run. But, something gets in the way. Some problem arises that suddenly jeopardizes your plans. Where once the coast was clear, now there are obstacles in the way.

Defining External and Internal Running Obstacles

Basically, there are two different kinds of running obstacles. Sometimes the obstacles are from *without*: external obstacles. Your child wakes up with a fever and you cannot leave her. An ice storm has left the roads impassable. Your running shoes catch fire. Okay—this last event is improbable, but I mention it just to illustrate the point that sometimes situations outside your control arise that make running impossible for you. You'll learn more about events of this sort later in the book, when we discuss issues runners face as a result of family commitments, injury, aging, or simply surprises that life tosses in the way.

This chapter focuses on obstacles to running that come from within: internal obstacles. These are the obstacles we create for ourselves. Whether you're a seasoned marathoner who puts in forty or more miles a week, a casual runner who's happy with a few 5Ks or 10Ks a week, or a newbie working to build a basic level of fitness before adding more miles to your routine, you will come face to face with motivational problems at some time or other. These dreaded sirens do their best to keep you in bed until it's just too late to squeeze in a run before work. They call to you in sweet, melodic voices, telling you that you ran just the other day—what's one missed run? In a seductive purr they remind you that you've had a busy day and deserve an evening off: you could pour yourself a glass of wine and unfold the newspaper you didn't have time to read before rushing to the office this morning. We've all heard these siren songs before. Let's look more closely at some of the common ones.

Examining Favorite Excuses Not to Run

Occasionally, runners find themselves in situations where excuses not to run are especially easy to find. They hang like ripe fruit from the branches, just waiting to be plucked. When these excuses dangle in front of your nose, they are almost impossible to resist.

Excuse Number One: Lousy Weather

I've been known to come up with some pretty creative excuses to avoid running when the weather is poor. Let's say I'm lying between warm sheets, next to my wife's warm body. The wind howls outside, causing branches to scratch against the window like mice clawing their way to the security of their nest. "Aren't you going running?" my wife asks, curling herself more tightly in the blankets.

"Well," I answer, "that was the plan, but I have a really busy day ahead and don't want to wear myself out."

"But you always say that running gives you energy," my wife responds. And, of course, she's right. One of the great benefits of running is that it does the exact opposite of wearing us out. I almost always run first thing in the morning. The rush a morning run gives me lasts well into the day, seeing me through the more tedious aspects of my job. The excuse I've just given my wife is lame, and she knows it. So . . . time to find another! "Actually, I'm meeting my boss for breakfast, and . . ." And what? I've started the excuse even before I can think how to end it. This is a sure sign that I'm fooling myself. I better think fast before . . .

"And what?" my wife asks. "You can't go to breakfast after running? You can't eat with other people after you run? You seem to do okay eating breakfast with me after you run."

"Well, I'm likely to be thirsty, and I'll drink a lot of water during breakfast."

"So?" she asks, quite reasonably.

"And so . . . and so . . . And so my boss will think I have a drinking problem. That's why I can't go running this morning." My wife stares at me as if she's just coming to realize that she's married a lunatic, and can you blame her? It's no secret that people are very good at rationalizing their decisions. The simple fact is that I don't *want* to go running in foul weather when I'm cozy in bed, and I'll make up all sorts of stories to get out of it.

Maybe you've never come up with excuses exactly like ones that I've tried, but I bet you've come up with some doozies of your own. There is never any shortage of reasons you can't run when the real reason is that you just don't feel like running in unpleasant weather. Here's where a Zen attitude can make the difference. Because Zen toughens your mind, because it creates a mind less vulnerable to temptations that are at odds with your plans to run, a little Zen philosophy can give you the boost you need when you find your motivation to run waning.

Excuse Number Two: Travel

As a professor, I travel quite a lot. It's not unusual for me to spend thirty-six hours in Chicago, where I'll deliver a lecture to a philosophy department, return home for a few days, and then fly to Vancouver, where I'll attend a conference for three days. If you travel too, then perhaps you're familiar with the extra burden that sometimes accompanies the thought of running while away from home. Perhaps your daily cycle has been thrown off by a time change. You're new to your locale and haven't the first idea which direction to run once you leave your hotel. Your diet, almost inevitably, is less healthy than the one you keep at home. All this change and uncertainty, at least for me, makes the thought of running much less appealing. What's a traveler to do? Zen can help you meet the extra difficulties that travel brings to runners. There are mental adjustments you can make that will help you overcome the unease that travel sometimes brings to running.

Excuse Number Three: Workplace Stress

Another motivation sap comes from the preoccupations and stress that we all take home with us from work. The greatest stress in my life comes from deadlines that seem forever looming. For me, these deadlines often involve chapters I've agreed to write for an editor who is putting together a book, or they might be for lectures that I've signed on to deliver in a month.

FROM THE MOUTHS *of Runners*

ERIC 24, OHIO "Excuses are easy. The main excuse I give is that it takes too much time. If it's a busy week, or a busy day, a forty-five-minute run, plus a shower and the post-run laziness, ends up being over an hour. Still, once I get that run in, I never regret the time it's taken. It's often the best part of my day."

Anxieties like these can drain your energy, making your feet feel like they weigh a hundred pounds each. When you feel like this, running is often the last thing you want to do, even though you might know, at some level, that a run would be the very best thing for you. Zen philosophy can teach you how to compartmentalize your worries.

Finding Motivation in Zen

Runners must often overcome those three internal obstacles in order to get their feet out the door and on the road. These are called *internal* obstacles because they arise from within. They come from our own weakness of will, or uncertainties, or anxieties. These anxieties can produce a feeling of malaise in anyone, and in runners this malaise manifests itself in a lack of desire to run. Let's now see how a Zen attitude can help you find your way through all three of these familiar challenges.

Because Zen teaches mental discipline, it can be used to toughen your mind, making your mind resistant to the excuses that so often lay waste to a runner's best-laid plans. The central concept that Zen offers for purposes like this is *mindfulness*. The practice of mindfulness will enable you to isolate the negative emotions that weaken your motivation, allowing you to avoid them.

Here's an example. Although I'm originally from New Jersey, I now live in Madison, Wisconsin. On days when I'm homesick, Wisconsin seems like one of the most inhospitable places in the world. Temperatures in the winter can dip to twenty below zero. That's without a wind chill factor. Summer days can top one hundred degrees, with humidity so high that even the trees look like they're perspiring. Believe me, if I want to use the weather as an excuse not to run, there are plenty of people who would never think to question my resolve.

I like to run, but that's not always enough on those bitterly cold winter mornings, when the sun is still hours from rising, when patches of ice on the sidewalk reflect the gleam of the streetlights. So, how do I get myself out of bed and onto the road? Here's where Zen comes in. Let's consider how a Zen attitude can help in this case.

Using Mindfulness to Change Your Attitude

So the wind screeches; snow blows against the window; you're snug beneath your blankets. You could sleep in, but this is a run you feel you need to do. Perhaps you're training, or perhaps you haven't run for a few days and you're worried that you'll begin to lose your hard-earned conditioning. But knowing the importance of the run isn't enough to get you out of bed today. You need to change your attitude.

Listing What's on Your Mind

The first step toward overcoming your motivational problem involves a heavy dose of introspection. Suppose that you are like me and find your resolve to run quickly fading when the weather turns nasty. Look into your mind and try to list the reasons you have for not wanting to run. The list might look like this:

1. It's dark.
2. It's cold.
3. I'm comfortable in bed.

This process of bringing to the front of your consciousness each thought and emotion you have is an example of what Buddhists call *mindfulness*. Being mindful is being attentive to what's going on in your mind. But, in fact, when you look more closely at what's on the list, you might notice that the first two items are of a different kind from the third item. Being dark and being cold aren't thoughts or emotions. Dark and cold are not things in your mind at all. They are things outside your mind. They are things in the world. On the other hand, being comfortable, the third item on the list, is something in your mind. Being comfortable is a way of feeling.

I hope this distinction between things in your mind and things outside of it is pretty intuitive. Obviously, things like tables, chairs, telephones, and snowstorms are not in your mind. What is in your mind, however, are *thoughts* about tables, chairs, telephones, and snowstorms. Being mindful means paying attention to your thoughts and emotions, and it is through mindfulness that we can overcome the thoughts and emotions that prevent us from running.

Distinguishing the World from Your Attitudes about the World

Thoughts and emotions aren't the only things in your mind. Your mind also contains memories that can affect the way you think about things outside your mind. For instance, suppose as a thirteen-year-old you had a bad experience with a doll. Maybe you were alone one night after watching a horror movie about dolls that came to life and attacked their owners with spoons. The movie terrified you, and as you climbed the stairs to your bedroom, you kept looking over your shoulder to assure yourself that no spoon-wielding doll was creeping up behind you. You entered your bedroom, turned down your bedspread, and there, on your pillow, was a doll your little sister had thoughtfully placed there for you. From that day on, you could never look at a doll without reliving, perhaps only subconsciously, the terror you felt seeing the doll laid out on your pillow.

The biases that result from our experiences in the world cause us to misperceive things outside our mind. This is what happened in the doll example. Because of your past experience, you continued to see dolls as frightening, dangerous, or disturbing. But let's say you pick up a doll today and consider it from a Zen perspective. The doll isn't frightening. You look at it again. What do you really see? What does the doll look like once you *see through* your prior experience with dolls? The doll looks like nothing more than stuffed cloth, with red yarn for hair and buttons for eyes. That's all there is to the doll. If it looks frightening, that's because *you* are adding something to the doll that isn't really there. This is obvious once you realize that other people enjoy dolls. They look at the same doll you see and, instead of recoiling as you might, they smile and take the doll into their arms. Properly speaking, the doll looks *neither* frightening nor cuddly. The doll looks like a doll. How you *see* the doll is a result of what's inside you—your memories and experiences.

ZEN **Practice**

Find something you have a strong aversion toward—such as a spider, mayonnaise, a photograph or painting, and so forth— and really look at it. Try to detach your feelings about the object from how the object really is. Determine how it is apart from your attitudes toward it.

Applying Mindfulness to Your List

Now let's look again at the three-item list of reasons not to run:

1. It's dark.
2. It's cold.
3. I'm comfortable in bed.

Again, the first two items on the list, dark and cold, are not things in your mind but things outside your mind. But, because the first step toward taking control of your mind is to sort out what is in it, you need to rewrite that list so that it contains only things in your mind. Here's a suggestion for how to do that:

1. I don't like the dark.
2. I don't like the cold.
3. It's comfortable in bed.

See what's happened to the original list? Where that list included things outside your mind, this list contains only things in your mind. Dark and cold have been replaced by attitudes you have toward dark and cold. Darkness is outside your mind, but your dislike for darkness is in your mind. Now we're making progress.

Breaking Attachments

Buddhists have a name for the biases we have, such as in the doll example. They call them *attachments*. Attachments are unusually strong commitments that we make to particular beliefs and desires, and they are often what stand in the way of happiness and success. In the doll example, you became attached to the idea that dolls are frightening. Once you understand that you are attached to this idea, breaking the attachment becomes easier.

To break the attachment, you must ask yourself why you are attached to the idea that the doll is frightening. By now, you should understand that the doll is in reality *not* frightening—it is you who makes it frightening. Breaking this attachment is as simple as recognizing that the doll is simply a doll. If it frightens you, this is not because of anything the doll is doing, or any way the doll appears. It's your choice to be frightened by the doll. So, stop! You can't always control what's going on outside your mind, but you often *can* control what's going on inside of it. See the doll as it really is, and you'll no longer be afraid of it.

Using Mindfulness to Help You Out of Bed

Now let's tackle the case that really matters here. How do you get yourself to run when the bed is warm and the weather is cold? You must first realize that you suffer from attachments that prevent you from seeing the world as it really is. You are attached to the ideas that you don't like the dark, that you don't like the cold, and that you're comfortable in bed. But, why don't you like the dark and the cold? Why do you feel so comfortable in bed? Dark and cold are not intrinsically bad things. Warm beds are not intrinsically comfortable things. You are the one who chooses to dislike dark and cold, and you are the one who chooses to enjoy warm beds. Somehow you've managed to attach yourself to the ideas that dark and cold conditions are to be avoided. But dark is simply dark; cold is simply cold. Don't let your attachment to the idea that you must avoid these things rule your life. The choice is yours. Let your attachments go. Get out of bed and face the world as it really is—not bad, not scary, not unwelcoming, just *as it is*.

Some of you might now be thinking, "Yeah, easy enough to say, but the problem is that dark and cold conditions *are* unpleasant. Beds *are* comfortable. That's why it's hard to make yourself get out of bed and run." Believe me, I hear you. Zen takes practice. Giving up your attachments is not always easy. Fortunately, as a disciplined runner, you're presumably not afraid of putting some effort into practicing. Remember when you first started to run and a mile seemed like an insurmountable distance? Then, when you were able to do a mile, a 5K run seemed impossibly far? Then, having mastered the 5K distance, you set your sights on a 10K distance that you never thought you could complete?

BUDDHA **Says**

In the sky, there is no distinction between east and west. People create distinctions in their own minds and then believe them to be true.

Zen training is hard. I didn't simply wake up one dark and cold morning with the realization that my dislike for the dark and the cold was a choice I had made, an attachment that I had created and was now allowing to control my life. Instead, having learned about mindfulness and attachments, I started small and worked my way up—just like you did when you first learned to run.

Practicing Mindfulness

Try this. There's probably a time of day that you don't like to run. I've already told you that I like to run in the mornings. Sometimes I just can't, and I'm forced to run in the late afternoon. Because I prefer morning runs, it's harder for me to get myself to run in the afternoon. This is true even when the weather is fine; even, in fact, when the afternoon is nicer than the morning was. Knowing this about myself, I decided to begin my Zen training by deliberately *not* running in the morning. I wanted to give myself an opportunity to overcome a *small amount* of adversity. I prefer not to run in the afternoon, but it's something I can do.

First Step: Separate Fact from Attitude

In my case, I listed all the reasons that I don't like to run in the afternoon. Here they are:

1. I feel tired after a day at work.
2. I like to relax when I come home from work.
3. I don't like having to run through rush hour traffic.

Now, make up your own list. Your list might be similar to mine, or maybe, unlike me, you like running in the afternoon but don't enjoy morning runs. That's fine. All I'm asking you to do now is come up with a list of reasons why you don't like to run at some given time of day. Remember to make the items on your list consist of only things in your mind—thoughts, feelings, emotions, and so on. Being mindful means concentrating on what's in your mind, not on what's outside it. We can control what's going on in our mind, but that's not always true of things going on outside it.

ZEN **Practice**

Come up with a list of reasons that you don't like to run at a particular time of the day. Once you have this list, think hard about each item, and try to separate the facts on the list, such as the fact that it is dark early in the morning, from your *attitude* about that fact.

Second Step: Identify Your Attachments

Next, I identified my attachments.

1. Attachment to the idea that I can't run when I am tired. The first reason I don't like to run in the afternoon is that I feel tired after work. But, why does this matter? Feeling tired should not by itself prevent me from running. I'm simply attached to the idea that I shouldn't run if I feel tired. I'm not saying that I'm not tired when I return home from work— I'm simply saying that being tired is by itself not a good thing or a bad thing: It's just the way I feel. I can choose to use it as an excuse not to run, or I can choose not to let it bother me. Of course, if I am so tired that I'm simply physically unable to run, that's a different matter. But that's never really true. I often spend the day sitting in front of my computer trying to write, or at a desk grading student papers. The fatigue I feel at the end of the day isn't the kind that makes my legs wobbly. I'm able to run; I just tell myself that because I feel tired I shouldn't run. But that's not true. What is true is that I'm attached to the idea that I shouldn't run if I feel tired. It's that attachment I need to toss aside. The same is true with the other items on the list.

2. Attachment to the idea that relaxing is better than running. I do like to relax when I come home from work. That's true. But it's not true that because I like to relax, I should not run. There's an attachment in there that I have to recognize. I'm attached to the idea that relaxing is preferable to running. But why is that? Relaxing is just that: relaxing. Relaxing is not intrinsically better or worse than running. If I prefer relaxing to running, that's my doing. I have convinced myself that I should prefer relaxation to running. The choice is mine.

3. Attachment to the idea that traffic is bad. And what of the rush hour traffic? The reality is that there is rush hour traffic in the afternoon. Is this bad? How could it not be, you might wonder. But if you're wondering this, you're missing the point about attachments. Rush hour traffic is nothing more than what it is: lots of cars making lots of noise. Whether this is bad or good depends on your attitude toward it.

After practicing mindfulness and identifying my attachments, I started running. Of course, the first thing I noticed was the rush hour congestion. My immediate reaction was disgust. "Ugh," I thought. "Why am I running now when I could avoid this by running in the morning?" It's not easy to give up your attachments. As soon as I caught myself taking a negative attitude toward the traffic, I had to remind myself that this negative reaction was my choice. I was in charge. If I chose to dislike the traffic, and if I allowed this to ruin my run, then I could do that. On the other hand, if I chose not to let the traffic bother me, or even allowed myself to enjoy the fact that I was moving faster than the cars on the road, then I could do that too. When I looked at the situation in terms of a decision I could make—a choice for which I was responsible—ridding myself of harmful attachments became much easier.

Facing Off Against Tougher Attachments

Once you've practiced losing your attachments to the thoughts and emotions that present you with small reasons not to run, you can move on to the big reasons that frequently sap your motivation to run. This is what I did. I worked on running in the afternoon—a small obstacle for me—and then I tackled a larger obstacle: inclement weather.

Breaking Attachments about Time of Day

As I've explained, first I made myself run in the afternoons until I was able to view dispassionately the ideas and feelings that initially made afternoon runs difficult for me. This didn't happen all at once, and on more than one occasion, after I thought I had kicked the habit, my old attachments returned to haunt me. Just when I thought I had liberated myself from the idea that relaxation was better than running, or that being tired meant I shouldn't run, the attachment would come back. I had to remind myself all over again that if relaxation seemed better than running, it was just because I *chose* to think of it as better. If being tired seemed to mean I shouldn't run, that was only because I had *decided* that was what being tired meant. In less than two months, I prevailed. I was able to run in the afternoons as easily as I could run in the mornings.

FROM THE MOUTHS *of Runners*

TRACEY 32, CALIFORNIA "I think it's bad to convince yourself that there is only one time of day that you can run. Instead, I make sure to carve out some time every day, even if it is in the dark at nine P.M."

Did this mean that I continued to run in the afternoons? No, I didn't. Morning runs are more convenient for me. Also, there are aspects of morning runs that I enjoy—features of morning runs—that are just not available in the afternoon. I like the quiet of the early morning. I like watching the sunrise. I like seeing fog hanging over the lake near my house.

Taking a Zen attitude doesn't mean you have to give up the joys in your life. I didn't make myself run in the afternoons to deprive myself of the pleasure that morning runs give me, but to train my mind to defeat harmful attachments.

Breaking Attachments about Weather

If running in the afternoon presented me with a small motivational burden, running in the rain posed a slightly larger one. When my alarm goes off I usually roll out of bed and look out the window in order to decide which running gear to wear. The sight of rain always dispirits me. I know I'm in for a struggle. So, how do I get myself out the door? First, I search my mind for the reasons I don't like to run in the rain. There are basically just two reasons:

1. I dislike getting wet.
2. I find the grey sky depressing.

Having practiced mindfulness, I then think about the attachments that are making it hard for me to run. I will get wet if I run in the rain. There's no denying that. But why is getting wet a bad thing? When I'm wet, I'm wet. That's it. That's all there is to it. Being wet is neither bad nor good. If I dislike getting wet, that's a choice I have made. In fact, I often make the opposite choice. Sometimes I like getting wet. This is why I go swimming, or sit in a hot tub. When do I hate getting wet and when do I like getting wet? Just when I choose to hate it or I choose to like it.

Why do I find the grey sky depressing? The grey sky is not, in and of itself, depressing. It's grey, and that's all it is. If I want to let the grey sky depress me, then it will. On the other hand, if I tell myself that grey is just a color, like blue or white or any of the other colors that the sky might be, it no longer saddens me.

Now, whenever I awake to rain, I put myself through the exercise I just described. Like running in the afternoon, getting myself to run in the rain took practice. The attachments that made it difficult for me to run in the rain still rear their ugly heads from time to time. But, over time, I've become much better at dispensing with them. I now find running in the rain much easier to do. In fact, I've even learned to enjoy these runs.

FROM THE MOUTHS *of Runners*

KATY 42, WISCONSIN "I don't actually mind running in the rain; in fact, my favorite runs of all start out with dry warm weather and progress through tentative raindrops and pleasing showers to soaking downpours. You don't really notice it's raining."

I sometimes see runs in the rain as a pleasant change from the ordinary. Instead of attaching negative attitudes toward getting wet and grey skies, I now attach positive attitudes to these things. Why not? I'm the one who has the power to choose how to think about them.

Creating a Recipe for Motivation

I think you see where I'm headed with all this. I first taught myself how to conquer the attachments that made running in the afternoon a chore for me. I then moved on to a greater challenge: I trained myself to run in the rain. Even though I have a harder time running in the rain than I do running in the afternoon, the same techniques work in both cases. You can use them, too.

First, practice mindfulness. Concentrate on the thoughts and emotions that prevent you from running. Second, figure out why you are attached to these thoughts and emotions and what you can do to rid yourself of these attachments. The recipe sounds simple, but it isn't. You really need to work hard to discover which thoughts and emotions are weighing you down, and then you have to work even harder to surmount your attachments to these thoughts and emotions. However, if you start with something not too difficult, you'll soon learn what it feels like to remove harmful attachments.

BUDDHA **Says**

A jug fills drop by drop.

Once you know this feeling, you're ready to move on to more entrenched attachments. In time, you'll find yourself having fewer motivational problems, even in extreme cases like the one I described earlier in this chapter, when the wind is howling, the snow is swirling, and daylight is hours away.

Using Zen for Travel Running

As I mentioned, I do a fair amount of traveling. Sometimes the trips are brief and I don't even bother to pack my running gear. I can survive thirty-six hours without running. But if I'm going to be away from home for more than two days, I'll want to run. At least, that's what I used to tell myself as I packed my suitcase: I rarely go more than two days without running, so why should that change just because I'm not at home?

But, these good intentions often did not amount to much. I can't tell you the number of times that I packed my shoes only to bring them home again unworn. There was something about being in a hotel in an unknown city, eating unfamiliar food, and adopting an atypical schedule that drained me of the desire to run. Every night I would set the alarm clock on the bedside table. Every morning the clock's beeping would wake me up. And then, and then, and then . . . I'd either fall back to sleep or grab the television remote to turn on a news program.

Traveling with Mindfulness

However, once I began to learn about Zen and to develop an understanding of mindfulness and attachments, I found I could change my attitude toward what I have come to call *travel running*. Mindfulness, remember, involves attending to your thoughts and emotions at any given moment. Now when I travel and find myself fighting the urge to go back to sleep or to watch television when I should be running, I make a mental list of all the thoughts and emotions that are weakening my resolve to run. Initially the list looked something like this:

1. I'm afraid that I might wander into an unsafe part of town.
2. I'm afraid I might become lost.
3. The time change (if there is one) makes me feel like I'm running at the wrong time.
4. I don't like running until I've had my oatmeal.

Your list might not be just like mine. In fact, I made up the fourth item. I don't like to eat anything before I run unless the run I've planned will exceed ten miles, but I do know people who swear they can't run unless they've had their oatmeal, or their yogurt, or their granola. For these people, travel running is out of the question unless they bring along their special running food and have a hotel room with facilities adequate for the food's preparation.

Dealing with Travel Attachments

The first thing to notice about this list is that not all the items present problems that we *should* try to detach ourselves from. When we engage in mindfulness and make ourselves aware of the fears and worries that prevent us from doing something, we shouldn't expect that our attachments to these fears and worries are always unreasonable. For instance, the second item on the list seems to be a good worry to have. I used to live in Philadelphia, and when runner friends from out of town would visit me, I would make sure they understood where it was safe to run and where running might put them at risk. There's no reason anyone should give up an attachment to the desire to run in safe places and to avoid risky places. This is just good sense.

FROM THE MOUTHS *of Runners*

RICK 46, ILLINOIS "The key to running while traveling is to find a good concierge or other knowledgeable person to point out a neat area. Hard to beat one hotel I stayed at near St. Louis, where upon finishing a nice run I was instantly handed a bottle of cold water and a plush towel."

Concerns about Safety

Fortunately, worries about our safety can be handled in other ways. If I'm going to be travel running in an unfamiliar city, I make a point of dropping by my local bookstore a week or so before my departure. There I'll look through various travel guides, making note of which areas of the city contain tourist attractions. Sometimes I can also access this information online.

Usually, these tourist areas are secure. Every city is interested in making itself safe for tourism. With this information in hand, I no longer have to worry about straying into risky areas when I run. Also helpful are conversations with others who have visited the city, or people you might be visiting in the city. Because my traveling is usually by invitation from people at a university, I almost always have hosts who can direct me away from the less savory areas of a city.

Concerns about Becoming Lost

What of the worry about becoming lost? If I know that I'm not going to stumble into a dangerous situation, I no longer think that becoming lost is a good reason not to run. I think the attachment to the idea that you must always know where you are is in fact harmful. Let's think about this. I know quite a few people who become very anxious when they stray from their intended path. Their worries are not about their personal safety. They're anxious no matter where they are when they become lost—cow pastures, Amish villages, desert islands. What is the source of this attachment to the idea that you must always know where you are?

The attachment seems to derive from another kind of attachment—a preference for the familiar. You feel comfortable in places you've been before and nervous in places that you've never seen and never intended to see. But, putting aside concerns about safety, there is no reason to prefer familiar locations to novel locations. One is a place you've been to before and the other is a place that you're visiting for the first time. There is nothing intrinsically better about places you've visited previously. If you find your old haunts preferable to locations you never intended to visit, this is a fact about you, not about the places themselves. You are the one who is causing your anxiety about being lost. You are the one who can prevent this anxiety.

RUNNING **Tip**

For running in terra incognita, try the site *www.mapmyrun.com.* Just type in the name of your travel destination and you'll find a street map on which you can plot runs of any distance. If you want, you can have the map display locations of water fountains, bathrooms, and hospitals. You can even overlay the map over a satellite image if you want to get a better picture of what the run has to offer. The site also gives you access to previously plotted runs if you want to see what other runners recommend.

Of course, this Zen approach toward concerns about becoming lost has its limitations. I have been assuming that being lost means simply being in a place that's new to you and where you did not intend to be. If being lost puts you in some danger, then this is a different and more distressing situation. For instance, you can be in real jeopardy if you've become lost in severe weather. Frostbite and hypothermia are concerns that runners in northern climates have to take seriously. Similarly, dehydration and heat stroke are real threats on scorching hot days. For safety's sake, you should probably reject attachments to concerns about becoming lost only when your travel running takes place within populated areas where, if necessary, you can always find someone to provide you with directions back to your hotel if your safety is at risk. As with fears about running in unsafe areas, fears of being lost make good sense when there is a chance of peril.

FROM THE MOUTHS *of Runners*

URIAH 39, ISRAEL "I love running while I'm traveling. I'll leave my hotel at six or seven A.M. and run through the still empty streets of a city I don't know. It's the quickest way to get acquainted with a new place: you get to see quite a bit in an hour of running around!"

When your concerns about becoming lost are legitimate, there are precautions you can take. The same travel books and online sites that can help you identify safe areas in which to run can also provide you with street maps that are often sufficiently detailed for runners' needs. While carrying along a map on a run is not ideal, you might take along a slip of paper with a list of street names to follow. At the very least, you can memorize the names of major streets or land-marks by which you can orient yourself should you become lost. Some Internet sites even allow you to plot your runs. These sites can also tell you the distance between points so that you can plan runs of specific lengths.

I hope I've said enough about the first two reasons on the list—fear for safety and fear of becoming lost—to help minimize the effect these reasons might have on your motivation to run while travel-ing. The next two items on the list are clear cases, I think, of letting attachments get the better of you.

Concerns about Changes in Your Running Schedule

The first issue is that you dislike running on a new schedule, and the second is that you have grown used to eating some favorite food before running. Many of the points I made earlier about how to train yourself to run during a time of day when you typically do not run apply to this first excuse as well. Why are you attached to the idea that your running time cannot vary? Why are you attached to the idea that a run that usually takes place at six o'clock Eastern Standard Time cannot happen at six o'clock Central Standard Time? Your body may not be used to running at different times, but the fact that you must run on a new schedule is by itself no reason not to run. Different times of day are just that—different times. If one time seems preferable to another, that's just because you have become attached to that idea.

Remember the doll? She's frightening only if you allow her to be. The same lesson is true here. A particular time to run is better than another only if you decide to see it that way. Once you clarify your attachment to these ideas that are making it hard for you to run, giving them up is that much easier.

Concerns about Changes in Your Diet

This last point is no less true of that "need" you have for that special oatmeal before a run. You don't really need that particular food. You have simply convinced yourself that you need that food. If you're hungry, some other food will do as well. Don't let an attachment to the idea that oatmeal (or whatever) is the only food you can eat before a run take control of your life. Once brought into the clear light of day, I think the folly of this attachment is obvious.

To summarize, travel running doesn't have to be harder than the running you do at home. Of course, travel running will not be the same as your routine running. Travel running takes place in unfamiliar locations, at unfamiliar times. Your body might be digesting different kinds of food than it's used to. But, you shouldn't let these differences discourage you from lacing up your running shoes. You're the one who has the power to decide whether to cling to old attachments that diminish the pleasure you can take from travel running, or whether to abandon these attachments in favor of new ones that can show you the joy of novelty that travel running promises. I've taken the second route, and I encourage you to give it a try.

Handling Stress with Zen

So far you've learned how a Zen perspective can help curb motivational problems that frequently befall even the most ardent runners. Sometimes these reasons are ordinary, having to do with inclement weather or changes in one's daily schedule. Other times, the reasons might be more specific. Now let's consider another source of motivational problems. These are the stresses and anxieties that nearly all of us face as a result of work-related responsibilities that fall on our shoulders. I'm referring to all those duties, deadlines, reports, meetings, and projects that make you groan.

I know I'm not the only one who wakes up some mornings and, as the workday ahead of me seeps into consciousness, wishes I could remain in bed for the rest of my life. Or, at least, until I retire. The busiest times in my life are at the ends of the semesters—December and May. At these times of the year I have stacks of papers and exams to grade, important conferences in which I am expected to participate, dreary department meetings I'm obliged to attend, and a normal load of paper deadlines I'm expected to meet. Just thinking about all these commitments can make my gut tighten.

BUDDHA **Says**

Peace comes from within. Do not seek it from without.

The effect that work-related stress can have on your psychological well-being should not be underestimated. People suffering from high anxiety will often change their diet, either over-eating or under-eating. Sleep is also a common casualty of stress. When I feel under tremendous pressure, I might go for a week or two with only four hours of sleep a night. Other people react to stress in the opposite way. They're always tired and find themselves napping at a time when they would ordinarily be productive.

Relieving Stress with Mindfulness

It should come as no surprise to you that running, as well as other forms of exercise, is actually an excellent antidote to job stress. This is something we all know. We run because it clears the head; it eases tension; it creates, however temporarily, a delicious euphoria. So, why can't we get ourselves to run when we most need to?

If you find this question hard to answer, you need to practice your mindfulness. Remember, I said earlier that mindfulness takes effort. Even though it's *your* mind, sometimes its contents are not always obvious. In fact, one of Sigmund Freud's great insights was that there are parts of our mind, our subconscious, that are closed off from our inspection. Following Freud's view, this is what explains Oedipus's behavior. Oedipus didn't realize that he was in fact attracted to his mother. If you had asked him whether he wanted to sleep with his mother, he would have responded with revulsion. He didn't know his own mind. Insofar as Freud is right about this, mindfulness can be an extremely difficult exercise.

Let's think some more about what's going through your mind when you're stressed out. What's going on in your mind that's diminishing your motivation to run? I've thought hard about this. Here's what I've come up with. When I'm feeling pressure from work, I tell myself that I can't run because I should be working. I become attached to this idea. I convince myself that any minute I don't spend working is a minute wasted. This, of course, is completely wrong. I know myself well enough to realize that a run as short as even half an hour energizes me. I'm far more productive throughout the day if I fit a run into my morning schedule than I am without the run. The half hour I spend running more than makes up for itself in increased efficiency throughout the day.

Still, knowing this and acting on this knowledge are two different things. My problem is convincing myself to run when I'm swamped with work, even though I know that the run will be good for me. This is an example of letting an attachment take control of our mind, even when we see it for the harmful attachment that it is. It's time to exorcise the nasty thing.

Listing Your Work Responsibilities

Begin by listing all the commitments, deadlines, and other responsibilities that are making you panic. Prioritize them, so that the most difficult or time-consuming or urgent come first on the list. This list will help relieve your tension. What once was an undefined mass of worries is now a precise and finite list of tasks.

Search your mind again. Are there any items on this list that you *fear* you are unable to accomplish? Are there items that you are *worried* you will not have time to complete? Does the list contain tasks that you especially *dislike*? Once you've identified the items on the list that cause fear, worry, and dislike, you're ready to deal with these harmful attachments.

Here's an example. At the top of my list of duties that drive me crazy is grading papers. Grading papers doesn't frighten me. Nor do I worry about running out of time to do all the work the task requires. I simply hate doing it. I'd rather do almost anything but grade papers. I may even prefer jumping from a bridge now that I'm thinking about it. So, I'm obviously attached to the idea that I very much dislike grading papers. Now what? I next ask myself whether the task of grading the papers will be easier if I allow myself to dislike it, or whether dreading the task will in fact make it even more horrible.

BUDDHA **Says**

We are what we think. All that we are arises in our thoughts. With our thoughts, we make the world.

I hope the answer to this question is obvious. Similarly, you can ask yourself whether fearing or worrying about a task is likely to make the task more or less arduous. Again, the answer should be obvious.

The point you must always bear in mind is that, whatever the task, your attitude toward the task does not change it. The task is what it is. However, although you may not be able to change the task, you can change your attitude toward the task. If I have sixty papers to grade, that's sixty papers to grade, and it will continue to be sixty papers to grade whether I loathe grading them or whether I accept the task with calmness. Why should I take the first attitude toward grading when I can take the second? Choosing not to hate grading papers is easy when I realize that an attachment to a negative attitude only makes grading harder.

By now, you should see the pattern of reasoning you can follow when, for whatever reason, your motivation to run flags. First, practice mindfulness. Plumb the depths of your mind to uncover exactly what thoughts, ideas, emotions, and so on are working against your plans to run. Second, analyze your attachments to these thoughts, ideas, and emotions. Why do you have these attachments? What put them there? Are they helping you or hurting you? If you take these steps—and, as I have been emphasizing, this requires practice and discipline—you'll find that the hurdles to your motivation are growing smaller, until one day you'll be able to clear them without even realizing that they're there.

CHAPTER 2
PREPARING FOR YOUR RUN

So you're ready to run. You want to run. You've overcome or never suffered the motivational obstacles we discussed in the previous chapter. You want to get in shape, stay in shape, lose weight, take your mind off of work, enjoy the outdoors, train for a marathon, cross-train. There are lots of reasons to run, and now one or more of those reasons has a hold on you. What next? Tie the laces and out you go, right? What could be simpler?

A Zen runner is able to find tranquility and joy in the act of running. This is a worthy goal, and one that you cannot achieve without adequate preparation. The goal will be beyond your reach if you are unable to rid yourself of negative emotions prior to running, or if you fail to anticipate obstacles that might impede your run. This chapter is about what you need to do *before* you start running in order to make your run a *Zen run*.

Maybe there was once a time when a decision to run could be easily translated into the actual act of running, but in today's high-tech, high-pressure, high-stakes world, a desire to run can often be far removed from the reality of running. Frequently there's just too much going on in life to make running—or any recreational activity, for that matter—something you can do on the spur of the moment. As a professor, I have the luxury of creating my own schedule, but I still have to plan my weeks carefully so that I can maximize my opportunities to run. If you have a fixed schedule, you may have even greater difficulty finding a good time to run. There are regular working hours to contend with, meetings, doctor appointments, PTA functions, book club gatherings, children's soccer practices, visiting in-laws, unexpected illnesses, and on and on. In short, there is rarely, if ever, such a thing as a spontaneous run.

Preparing to Run

With a life full of responsibilities, you need to plan your running carefully. You need to find times when it is easy to run, but you also need to be ready to seize an opportunity to run if and when one comes along. You need to think about family dynamics so that you don't have to choose between running and a relationship—I know people whose marriages nearly ended because they could not find a way to fit their running needs with their family's needs. You also need to know where to run. Given how difficult it can sometimes be to find a time to run, you want to make the most of the running opportunities you get. This means that you don't want to end up following a bus for several miles, having to wash the taste of diesel exhaust out of your mouth when at last you find your way out of the fog. You must also think carefully about how to dress appropriately for the run. You'll want to be wearing shoes that fit properly, and, depending on how far you're going, may even want to be sure that you've applied petroleum jelly to the places where your clothes may chafe against your skin.

Let's look at how a Zen perspective can simplify, facilitate, and make gratifying the various tasks involved in running preparation. At the same time, we will work toward how to make the time you spend running more peaceful and relaxing. Again, I hope to take you a step closer toward running the Zen way. An obvious place to start is at home.

Running When You Have a Family

By far the greatest challenge to running that I have ever faced was achieving and maintaining the delicate balance between my need to be out on the road and my desire to be a fully participating, loving, and loved member of my family. And my advice applies even if you don't have a family, or if your family is 100 percent behind your running. Unless you are a hermit living in the mountains of Idaho, it's likely that your desire to run sometimes inconveniences people who care for you and that, in time, hurt feelings will boil over into outright resentment. Preparing to run in a Zen way can help prevent this from happening.

Dealing with Family Tensions

A major reason for the tensions that often appear between runners and their families comes from differing perceptions about the role running plays in a runner's life. Many dedicated runners see their activity as an essential part of their lives, as a pursuit that brings spiritual and physical fulfillment. Their families may not understand this, thinking instead that running is no more than a hobby or an escape from the duties of family life. So, the bad news is that runners and their families can have different ideas about the meaning or significance of running. The good news, at least from a Zen perspective, is that the conflict arises in part from your *attitude* toward running. I say that this is good news because Zen is all about understanding and controlling one's attitudes, whether about running or other things. Zen can teach you how to focus your mind so that you can perceive the world more clearly. From this clearer vantage, you will have an easier time appreciating the nature of the conflict that running sometimes creates between you and your family, and once you possess this appreciation, you will have an easer time resolving this conflict.

Using Mindfulness to Resolve Family Tensions

In Chapter 1, we practiced an exercise in mindfulness when we learned that a crucial step in overcoming motivational obstacles is recognizing that these obstacles arise from *within*. They creep from deep within our own minds like nasty critters from a swamp. However, once we *see* our own mind—once we understand that these monsters are of our own making—we are in a position to battle them more effectively.

Mindfulness is also a first step in resolving the conflict that running can create between you and your loved ones. You cannot hope to address this conflict unless you understand how it arises, and to do this you must arrive at a state of clarity regarding your attitudes toward running. However, mindfulness is only a first step. We also need to think about the Buddhist practice of *right effort* in order to prepare most effectively against the negative emotions that running sometimes stirs up in its wake. All in good time. A Zen runner is, after all, a patient runner.

BUDDHA **Says**

To enjoy good health, to bring true happiness to one's family, and to bring peace to all, one must first discipline and control one's mind.

Engaging in mindfulness requires that you meticulously scrutinize your attitudes, beliefs, and desires. Here's a question that I want you to subject to mindfulness right now: Why do you run? What makes you take time away from a family or loved ones who, on occasion, would rather have you by their side, in order to spend hours doing something that you don't *have* to do? My hunch is that many of you have not really thought about this question, or have not thought deeply about this question. Here are some answers to the question that strike me as inadequate or unreflective:

1. I run because I like running.
2. I run because I like being in shape.
3. I run because it makes me feel good.

What's wrong with these answers? They hardly justify the risk of damaging one's relationship with loved ones. Remember we are imagining a situation where your desire to run is at odds with the needs of your family. Now consider the three answers again.

The first states something that may be true for most runners (although I do know runners who profess not to like running), but it is nevertheless flimsy. There are probably lots of things you like. Maybe you like watching television, or reading novels, or attending concerts. Would you plan to do these things regularly if you knew that doing them would lead members of your family to resent you? Probably not. Of course, we all deserve some time off. Zen does not require that you give up pleasures, although it does warn against excess. But if your only reason to run is for the pleasure it gives you, surely you should not plan to do so several times a week if this means trouble at home, or you should not resist plans for family activities in the future because they might conflict with plans to run. I know runners who do just this, and I wonder how long their families can endure this treatment.

FROM THE MOUTHS *of Runners*

WADE 52, INDIANA "As long as I am back from my run before the day begins for everyone else, there is no problem. That's why early-morning runs save marriages."

The second and third answers—that you run because you like to be in shape, or you run because it makes you feel good—also just aren't good enough. Imagine saying them if your spouse asked you to stay in and help care for two sick children on a Saturday morning: "Sorry, honey, but I really like being in shape" or "Sorry, dear, but running makes me feel good." It just doesn't cut it. There are occasions when your plans to run must simply give way to more important obligations.

However, many of the hard feelings that arise between runners and their families come from the runner's own confusion about why running is meaningful. If runners are uncertain of their own attitude toward their passion, how can they explain themselves to their family? Zen can help you understand why running matters so much to you, and so can be a first step in easing tensions that running creates between you and your family.

Defining the Personal Value of Running

Once you get past these superficial answers to the question about why you run, I think you'll hit on something closer to the truth. Let's start with something with which most runners would agree. Running, for a committed runner, is *not* a leisure activity. It's not like reading a trashy novel, spending the afternoon at the theater, or solving a crossword puzzle. It's not something we do (just) because we like doing it, or (just) because it keeps us in shape, or (just) because it makes us feel good. But, on the other hand, running is also not work. It's not something we do because we have to earn a living; it doesn't create anxiety in our lives or make us wish for a vacation.

Running, for a serious runner, falls into some third category—neither work nor play. If I'm unable to run for an extended period of time, I become listless, moody, and (so I'm told) grumpy. Situations that once seemed tolerable or even pleasant become a burden and a source of unease. We'll discuss how to cope with running withdrawal in a later chapter, but for now the point is that running is not on a par with those activities that we do just for the pleasure of doing them.

The best analogy I've come up with to describe what running means to me is sleep. Sleep isn't really a leisure activity because it is necessary for our well-being. We can't live without sleep. This is how many runners feel about running—we can't live without it. Running deprivation for runners is every bit as real and damaging as sleep deprivation. Unfortunately, as when we are sleeping, while we are running we are not able to contribute in any meaningful way to the needs of those who depend on us.

ZEN **Practice**

Come up with your own reasons for why you like to run. Try to decide how important these reasons are to you. What sacrifices are you willing to make to act on them?

In sum, mindfulness reveals that runners run less because of the pleasure it gives them than because of some need that it fulfills. It's a need just like sleep is a need. If everybody recognized this, the world would be a beautiful and peaceful place. Alas, non-runners take a different view of things, and this, I believe, is the primary source of friction between runners and their families. For non-runners, the act of running falls into the leisure category: it's not something that's physically necessary, like sleep, and it's also not something that runners have to do for economic reasons, like work. From this perspective, when runners tell their families that they can't join them for a weekend morning's outing to a zoo, church, or park, the announcement seems nothing less than evidence of wanton selfishness. "What do you mean you can't spend time with us?" Family members may ask with wide-eyed incredulity. "You can run some other time, but we're here, together, now!"

It's a good question, and one that should give pause to any runner who cares deeply for his or her family. Mindfulness helps reveal the nature of the problem. You have an obligation to your family and a desire to be with them. You also *need* to run, but your family perhaps does not understand this. This is a recipe for trouble. This is also a good time to avail yourself of the Buddha's teachings.

Recognizing the Causes of Suffering

When desires and needs clash, when the satisfaction of one is not possible without disregarding the other, something must give. This is true whether the clashing desires are your own or whether your desires conflict with others'. This battle of desire produces what Buddhists call *dukkha*, which, roughly translated, means "suffering." Suffering, of course, can take many forms—from the physical discomfort of impacted wisdom teeth to the mental anguish of grief. *Dukkha* refers to these sorts of torments, but it is especially focused on the kind of suffering that results from having desires for things that one simply cannot acquire. When I was a child, I desperately wanted to be able to fly. I don't mean that I wanted to be a pilot of an airplane, or that I wanted to strap myself to a hang glider and launch myself from a cliff. I wanted to fly. Like Superman. I wanted to lift my arms above my head and just *take off.* You will not be surprised to learn that my efforts went unrequited. In fact, I was no closer to flying after one thousand attempts than I was after the first. This was one of my first tastes of unadulterated *dukkha*. I wanted something I could not have and could *never* have. Recognition of this fact, slow as it was in coming, was heartrending for me. But, of course, thwarted desires are a fact of life.

Whether it is the desire to fly, or the desire to run whenever you'd like without having to worry about the needs of your family, the reality remains: we can't always get what we want.

The Buddha knew about desires of this kind. After all, he was human too. In his teachings, he spoke of the need to rid oneself of the negative emotions that arise from the inability to satisfy one's desires, whether these be silly desires, like wanting to fly, or more serious ones, like wanting to engage in activities that are likely to cause strife in one's family. The Buddha taught that the practice of *right effort* was necessary to eliminate the harmful emotions that emerge from thwarted desires. Let's now see how right effort can assist you in dealing with the sort of tension that comes from desiring incompatible ends: the freedom to run whenever you want and the desire to be there for your family or loved ones whenever they need you.

Understanding Right Effort

Right effort is the Buddhist name for the activity that turns negative emotions into positive ones. The goal of right effort is thus to alleviate *dukkha*. An example will help show how right effort is supposed to work. A while back I showed up at the airport expecting to fly to Switzerland only to find that my flight was delayed by four hours. This delay meant that I'd miss a connection, which meant that I'd be a day late for a conference I had been looking forward to attending. I'm sure you're familiar with this kind of situation—you don't have to travel often to experience it. So, I now found myself with a much longer trip ahead of me, and with less time at the destination than I had hoped to have.

One reaction to this turn of events would involve anger, frustration, irritation, and perhaps a temporarily soothing release of obscenities directed at ticketing agents, security personnel, and airline officials. Notice, however, that this reaction to the bad news would do absolutely nothing to change it. The flight would still depart late, the connection would still be missed, and the time at the desired destination would still be curtailed. On the other hand, the reaction would anger a number of people, and perhaps would cause an escalation to more serious difficulties.

A different reaction, and one for which I opted, would be to think of my four hours' extra time on the ground as an opportunity to browse a bookstore, have a beer while I read sections of the newspaper that I don't usually have time for, make a few phone calls, and put some more thought into the paper I would soon present. This reaction shows right effort at work. The idea of right effort is to replace negative emotions with positive ones. This idea makes a great deal of sense when, as in this situation, your actions can make no difference to the situation you are in. Nothing I could do would make my flight leave on time. The choice was thus mine to react negatively to the change in plans or positively.

BUDDHA **Says**

The mind is everything. What you think you then become.

Perhaps it is curious, once pointed out, that people *choose* to be angry or sullen or irritated. Why would anyone choose an unhappy emotion if it were possible to choose a happy one? Why, when forced to spend more time in an airport than you planned, react with a flash of anger rather than a shrug of your shoulders? The plane is late. The connection will be missed. On top of these misfortunes you can add another—a burst of anger that is likely only to worsen the situation—or you can instead accept your fate and look for ways to make the most of it.

Casting away negative thoughts and replacing them with positive ones is not always easy. In fact, it is one of the hardest skills for anyone to learn. Buddhists dedicate hours of the day just to develop this ability. *Zen*, which means meditation, is all about training the mind to succeed in right effort—to succeed in tossing out negative and harmful emotional states and replacing them with positive feelings and thoughts.

Putting Mindfulness and Right Effort Together

You should be able to see now how *mindfulness* and *right effort* complement each other. The goal of mindfulness is to become fully aware of the thoughts one is having, and of the emotions one is experiencing. As an example of mindfulness, I might carefully examine the reasons I am upset to have a delayed departure. As I place each reason under the mental microscope of mindfulness, I can detach myself from it. I can imagine the tedium of extra time in the airport, the disappointment that I'll be late for my conference, as things with substance—items with weight—that I can pick up and throw away. Then, using right effort, I can replace all my negative beliefs and feelings with positive and reassuring thoughts. In this way, I can squelch my anxieties and worries. My mind becomes tranquil, like the surface of a puddle after the rain has stopped. At any rate, that's my goal.

Applying Mindfulness and Right Effort in the Family

Let's now return to the *dukkha* that comes from wanting to run, *needing* to run, and simultaneously wanting and needing to be a dedicated member of your family. The mindfulness is already behind us. At this point we have a more precise and realistic grasp of the mental attitudes that are in conflict with each other. On the one hand, we recognize that running is not something we do merely for the joy it brings. The desire to run is more like the desire to sleep—something we must do. On the other hand, the desire to keep peace in the family—to be a loving and devoted spouse, parent, child, sibling—is also very real. We need to pursue some *right effort* to find a way out of this quandary.

The first step is to use mindfulness to isolate the negative emotions that this clash of desires is almost certain to create. You value running, and perhaps you resent your family for not perceiving it in the same light that you do. Whereas they think of running as a leisure activity, you recognize that it means more to you than that. Thus, you might feel hurt or exasperated that your family does not treat your desire to run with the gravity you think it deserves. But you also desire to make your family happy, to be an integral part of its functioning. Maybe you feel guilty that you cannot do this *and* spend as much time running as you would like. We now have before us a list of negative emotions to consider: resentment, hurt, guilt. Just knowing that these feelings go through your mind on various occasions is the first healthy step to eliminating them.

Handling Feelings of Hurt and Resentment

Right effort asks you to go a step further than simply recognizing these negative emotions. You must try to replace them with positive feelings. Instead of resenting your family for not appreciating what running means to you, you can focus on your good fortune at having a family that wants you to be with them. For many people, having a family that loves them is the ultimate happiness. You should never take your family's love for granted. Wouldn't you rather be part of a family that would like you to spend more time with them than less? The day my family tells me that they'd rather I go for a run than spend time with them is not a day I care to see.

Instead of feeling hurt that your family does not seem to recognize the significance of running in your life, you can feel content that you have a need that, compared to many others, is relatively easy to satisfy. You can be glad that you are addicted to something that, except in extremes, is good for you. You needn't think hard to come up with a list of addictions that are far worse for you than running. So, rather than being hurt by your family's apparent inability to understand the nature of your commitment to running, you can take joy in the fact that you have something special: a need that is at once relatively easy to satisfy and wholesome.

Handling Feelings of Guilt

What about your guilty feelings for not always being available for your family? There are two kinds of guilt, one bad and the other good. Bad guilt is the kind you feel toward some action you have taken (or not taken) despite not being culpable for the action (or lack of action). If you feel guilty for running over your neighbor's dog even though he dashed into the street in front of you, leaving you no time to stop the car, this is bad guilt. In this situation, you might feel sorrow that the dog is dead and that your neighbor is unhappy, but you should not feel guilty. There was nothing you could have done to prevent the terrible outcome. Feeling guilty will only compound the bad that is already in abundance.

Good guilt is the kind that tells you that you need to make amends for actions that have caused distress and that you could have prevented. If you recklessly trample through your neighbor's cherished tulip bed and feel no guilt for doing so, you have a problem. If you don't feel guilty about harms you have caused through negligence or thoughtlessness, then I would wager that you are not a person who cares much about other people. You probably would not feel guilty about leaving your family to go running, and, on the bright side, you would probably have nothing about which to feel guilty because your family might be glad to see you go in any case.

FROM THE MOUTHS *of Runners*
ERICA 36, AUSTRALIA "My husband always complains when I go out for a run because he thinks I am obsessed. But I know that he's proud of me for keeping in shape."

Which kind of guilt—good or bad—do you feel when your choice to run entails a choice not to participate in some family event? It's not bad guilt, because your run is not unavoidable and you are not unable to help yourself. Instead, it is good guilt that you feel. You realize that you can, without too much trouble, change your behavior so that you are more available to your family. Even if you are addicted to running, and recognize that the need for running resembles the need for sleep, this does not mean that you must be inflexible about the times you choose to run or about the number of runs you need to take each week.

I think what Zen teaches us in this case—what right effort guides us to do—is to seek a compromise with our family that leaves us with no reason to feel guilty.

Using Zen to Find a Compromise

You might think that you have already compromised enough, or that compromise is impossible given the various obligations in your busy life. But you should by now have some idea how to think about these matters from a Zen perspective. Ask yourself why you must run on Saturday mornings rather than Sunday mornings, or why you have to run at eight A.M. rather than seven A.M. I think that questions like these will reveal attachments, in the sense I discussed in the previous chapter, to desires and beliefs that you need to release. Attachments are not healthy. Unreflective commitment to beliefs and desires is bound to lead to negative feelings. With some mindfulness and right effort, you will be able to isolate exactly which beliefs and desires are preventing compromise, and, thereby, causing discord.

Although all families differ just as all people do, perhaps the story of how I overcame the troubles that my running needs were causing in my family will be of help to you. There was a time in my life soon after my second child was born that I was especially busy. My "tenure clock" was more than halfway through, meaning that I had just a few more years to write and publish as much as possible to improve my chance of receiving tenure. I spent a lot of time read-ing, writing, and simply staring at my computer monitor waiting for good ideas to come to mind. All of these activities, you might have noticed, took place in a chair. Chairs are no place for a runner. By the end of a nine- or ten-hour stint on my butt, I just had to run.

BUDDHA **Says**

Do not dwell in the past and do not dream of the future.
Concentrate the mind on the present moment.

My wife, however, had a different view of what I had to do. She spent her days chasing after an energetic two-year old while also trying to do laundry, prepare meals, and nurse a newborn. She wanted me home. She wanted a break. She resented, quite reasonably, whatever running I did, and I resented not having an opportunity to do anything but work and help with the children. On those occasions where I could sneak out for a run, I would come home feeling guilty about what I had done.

Obviously the situation was unhealthy and matters were not going to improve on their own. Here's what I did to repair things. I first took the Zen step of mindfulness, asking myself the sort of questions I asked earlier in this chapter. Why do I feel the need to run? What are the causes of the resentment and guilt I am feeling? How, using right effort, can I rid myself of these negative emotions? With what positive emotions can I replace them?

After searching my mind for answers to these questions, I was in a far better position to have a serious talk with my wife about our differing needs and priorities than I would have been in before practicing mindfulness and right effort. Knowing more precisely what I was thinking and why put me in a better position to move us toward a resolution. The solution turned out to be pretty simple. Mindfulness showed me that I was feeling very anxious about my impending tenure decision. I had become attached to the idea that my case was weak. Using right effort I realized that this worry was in fact distracting me. Nothing positive could come of it. Instead of worrying, I told myself that I was fortunate to have two years left to strengthen a case for tenure that was already pretty strong.

> **FROM THE MOUTHS** *of Runners*
>
> **JIM 54, NEW JERSEY** "With our second child, I received a baby jogger on Father's Day. Later I received a basket to attach to the jogger, and then I could 'run' errands during my runs, on the way home from the runs, whenever necessary. It was good to feel that I could run and help my family at the same time."

I next considered the resentment I felt toward my wife for wanting me to go on child-duty as soon as I returned home from research-duty. I reminded myself that my wife was not interested in punishing me. I was in fact very fortunate to have a wife who was willing to put her career on hold in order to raise our beautiful children.

In brief, right effort put me in a Zen frame of mind that made compromise easy. Compromise is *always* difficult when you approach it while harboring negative emotions. You can't help but feel dissatisfied or cheated if you enter a compromise with the attitude that anything short of exactly what you want is not enough. In the end, my wife and I hit on a solution that worked fine. If I just took one hour off from my research in the late morning to give my wife a break, she would have the strength and patience to make it through the rest of the day. Because this hour with the children meant I wasn't in a chair all day long, my desperation to run at day's end became less acute. I still ran, but not as often. The break in my workday actually helped to recharge my brain so that afternoons became more productive than they had been before the compromise.

I do not wish to give the impression that mindfulness and right effort can solve every difficulty a person faces. However, the practices of mindfulness and right effort will move you closer to solutions than you would get without them.

Choosing Your Path

Developing an understanding with your family about what running means to you and about how your need to run can be coordinated with your family's needs is probably the most important step you must take before heading out the door. You'll find no peace in your runs if feelings of resentment and guilt always accompany them. But if you want to get the most from your runs—and you probably do given how difficult it is to squeeze activities like running into our days—you will want to think about the route you will take before you get to the end of your driveway. There's nothing sadder than a run squandered; you don't want to make this mistake!

But what does it mean to "make the most" of a run? Zen running, as discussed earlier, is a special kind of running. We'll delve more into this in the fourth chapter, where we talk about turning your running into a form of meditation. For now, you need to understand that the goal of Zen running is to obtain peace of mind.

Obviously, if you feel more anxious or worried by the end of a run than you did at the start, you won't run. You *shouldn't* run. But this is all the more reason to take a few precautionary steps to ensure that your running path is also a carefree path.

BUDDHA **Says**

It is better to travel well than to arrive.

I'll assume that most of your running takes place in a neighborhood with which you are familiar. If you live in a city, you face special challenges and you need to think even harder about the route you'll take than runners who live in rural or suburban areas. In the next chapter, I will discuss how Zen can help you to deal with the complexities and anxieties that too frequently surface when running in a city. In any case, the following information should make sense wherever you happen to run—it's just harder to apply in a city.

By now you are familiar with the fundamentals of mindfulness and right effort. These practices are useful for draining from your mind negative feelings that bring you down. Happiness would be forever elusive if you let your darker thoughts rampage unchecked through your psyche. Mindfulness helps you identify these thoughts—to put them in your sight. Right effort redirects your thoughts, pointing them in positive directions. But, if you have tried your hand at mindfulness and right effort, you will have noticed that these activities are not easy. They require concentration. The more distractions you face, and the more negative feelings you accumulate, the harder these mental exercises become.

Finding the Positive Path

This difficulty of mindfulness and right effort suggests that you look for certain things in a running route. To ensure that your run will be as joyful and untroubled as possible, you will want to plan a path where you'll have the least need to apply mindfulness and right effort. Running while at the same time trying to locate and suppress disturbing thoughts is a lot harder than running while at the same time trying to chew gum (which is discouraged)! This means that you must take care to choose a path where you are least likely to confront negative thoughts.

Here's a technique you might find helpful. Imagine that your mind is a smooth pool of water, and ask yourself what is likely to upset this stillness. Alternatively, imagine that your mind is a choppy pool of water, and then ask yourself what you must do in order to still the waves. Either way, the goal is the same. You are searching for tranquility. Next, because you're familiar with your home turf, try out some different routes in your head. Close your eyes and do your best to bring these different routes to life. Ask yourself how you feel running them. Do you inwardly cringe when you imagine crossing a busy highway or passing a noisy construction site? Do the imagined sounds of bird song in the park at the end of the block cause your shoulders to relax and your breathing to deepen? This kind of virtual running can spare you from hassles and irritations that you may have encountered in your real runs.

Although I do not doubt that some people would rather run through noisy and dusty construction sites than they would through sun-dappled forests on paths softened with pine needles, I do believe that some running paths are naturally more conducive to Zen running than others.

> **FROM THE MOUTHS** *of Runners*
>
> **SHANNON 27, TEXAS** "I like running routes that are divided into distinct segments. For example, I have a route now where I run through downtown Madison for two miles. The next mile or so is on a road in the Arboretum, then I run for a few miles in trails, and I turn around to do the same route back. Having the run segmented into distinct parts makes it easier for me to stay focused. I can concentrate on what I'm feeling rather than on where I'm going."

Try, if you can, to incorporate into your running routine paths that will take you close to water. Water has always seemed to have a pacifying effect on the human mind, and you should take advantage of this if you can. If you like to run at dawn or dusk, look for a route where you will be able to see the sun rising or setting. The beauty of the sun hovering just above the horizon, painting the sky with purples and oranges, never fails to unburden my mind. I also quite like a route where I can climb and descend long rolling hills. The undulations in the terrain look from the distance like great sea waves, and this relaxes me in the same way that a glimpse of the actual sea might.

Of course, you know yourself best. Perhaps none of these suggestions grab you. Experiment with a variety of routes. You might even find that running beside a highway is something that brings unexpected pleasures. Some runners I know tell me that the roar of the highway reminds them of waves breaking on a beach, and they look forward to a run at rush hour when the "surf" is at its heaviest.

Dressing for the Run

One final thing that you need to consider before heading out the door is whether you are adequately dressed for whatever weather you might encounter on your running route. Naturally, the clothing you choose should be appropriate for the climate in which you run. In warm weather you should wear clothes made of fabric that "wicks." The last thing you need to carry with you on a run is your own perspiration! Wicking fabrics get rid of perspiration quickly. Otherwise, wet clothes add extra weight and chafe against sensitive areas. Cold weather runs (in Wisconsin my limit is twenty below zero) require layers of clothing. On your upper body try wearing a wicking long-sleeve shirt, a wicking short-sleeve t-shirt, a thicker running top, and then a wind-resistant GOR-TEX shell over all these layers. On the bottom try wearing shorts, followed by tights, followed by a wind-resistant nylon or GOR-TEX pant. No sweats. No fleeces. These become too heavy and actually provide too much warmth. Be sure to wear mittens—not gloves—in really cold weather. Your fingers will need to be in contact with each other to remain warm. Gloves only isolate the fingers, allowing each to freeze on their lonesome. For colder runs you may also want to wear a fleece turtle to keep your neck and chin insulated, and a fleece or wool cap that covers your ears. Ears are usually the first parts of the body to suffer frostbite, so be sure not to forget about these flappy appendages.

Keeping It Simple

Everything regarding dressing for your run is common sense. But when shopping for new running gear, try to keep in mind the Zen predilection for simplicity. Zen is about simplifying your life. A Zen mind is uncluttered. It's like an attic that has been emptied, dusted, and swept.

FROM THE MOUTHS *of Runners*

ARGY 48, PENNSYLVANIA "Running is the simplest form of exercise. You put on your shoes and step outside. What can be easier than that?"

The challenge to the Zen practitioner is to keep that attic clean. As tempting as it is to throw boxes of junk into the attic rather than sorting through them and finding better homes for the useless items they contain, doing so will only create future work. The same is true of the mind. You might be tempted to leave unexamined many of the negative emotions that afflict you. Perhaps certain thoughts cause you anxiety or pain, so you convince yourself that you'll get around to thinking about these things later. Don't do this. The more negative emotions you accumulate in your mental attic, the harder it will be to clear and clean when the time comes that it can simply hold no more.

The Zen rejection of gratuitous materialism is in part a reflection of this desire to keep the mind's contents to a minimum. For example, if I have two cars rather than one, I also have twice the worry that comes with owning one car. I now need to insure both cars, maintain both cars, and shelter both cars when I'm not using them.

There are twice the number of scratches, dings, flat tires. In general, the more one possesses, the more headaches one incurs as a result. Keep this in mind when you are shopping for running attire. When I go to purchase shoes, or shorts, or even mittens, I spend the first ten minutes in the store trying not to hyperventilate from the staggering variety of choices I confront. There are probably fifty kinds of running shoes that would suit my needs. The differences between them are mainly superficial. Whether the shocks in the heels are exposed or hidden makes no difference. Whether the stripe on the shoe's side is a swoosh that points up or down or is red or gold is not going to affect your performance.

RUNNING **Tip**

If you have trouble with your shoes coming untied while you run, try this. When you tie your shoes, put the "rabbit" into its hole twice. This knot will not let go, and, unlike a double knot, it unties with a single pull.

A long time ago I found a line of shoes that works fine for me. I have stuck with it. This is in the spirit of Zen. If you have found a product that works for you, don't let the flash or name brand of another product tempt you from what you know has worked in the past. Also, don't assume that the more expensive product is the better product.

A Zen attitude toward running gear encourages you to think about what you minimally need in order to have a comfortable run. Whether the product carries a particular label, or is a particular color, or is what everyone else is wearing, should be irrelevant.

You need to experiment with different products and find those that work for you. Of course, this carries an initial start-up cost. Those first mittens or first shoes might not be quite right. The shorts you buy might chafe. The sleeves on the shirt might flop around in a way that you don't like. But, once you've hit on a product line that's good for you, stick with it. Advertisers will try to convince you that you cannot possibly be comfortable or perform well without their latest and technologically most advanced apparel. Don't believe it. The purpose of advertising is to convince you that what you presently have isn't good enough. Sometimes this will be true, but usually not. Don't clutter your attic unnecessarily.

Lacing Up!

Time to get out there! If you've absorbed the Zen-inspired lessons to this point, you should be prepared for your run. Mindfulness and right effort have helped you make the compromises with your family that are sometimes necessary when your running schedule is at odds with your family's needs. Careful reflection on which running routes are more likely to contribute to your sense of calm should help make your running more joyful. Finally, if, when choosing your running apparel, you listened to your body's needs rather advertisers' promises, you will be moving in comfort. Remember: your goal is to make the most of your running. If you heed this advice, those negative emotions that can sometimes prowl uninvited into your run—those feelings of resentment that conflicts with your family might cause, or those annoyances that come from having chosen a bad route, or the physical discomfort that results from poor choices in running gear—are far less likely to make their malevolent presence known. A little bit of Zen preparation, and your running is sure to be more fulfilling.

CHAPTER 3
OVERCOMING OBSTACLES ON YOUR PATH

Very few of us have the good fortune to choose where we will live. Gone are the days, if such days there ever were, when you could look at a map, find what appears to be a beautiful spot, and declare with unreserved confidence: "This is where I shall live." With apologies to the Rolling Stones, you can't always live where you want. I've known people who complain incessantly about the cruel twist of fate that has landed them in a small lifeless town in the Midwest, or a congested metropolitan area on the East Coast, or a polluted and hazy city on the West Coast. As some people tell it, they'd prefer a life behind bars to the life in their present location. They see themselves as trapped. A job, a family, an ex-spouse with whom they share children, and so on, is anchoring them to the worst place in the world just as surely as a ball and chain.

It's tempting to feel a twinge of sorrow for the tellers of these tales. Not because their perceptions are incorrect. No doubt some environments are more conducive to peaceful and easy living than others.

FROM THE MOUTHS *of Runners*

JENNIFER 36, OHIO "We've chosen which neighborhood we would like to live in for three cities now based on accessibility to nice running routes. Do I have to cross major roads? Are there trails close by? Access to emergency bathrooms? It has served us well. I don't know how I could live without having a peaceful place to run."

But no place, probably not even prison, could be as bad as these tortured souls make their hometowns out to be. I feel for these people not because they live in one of Dante's nine circles of hell, but because they have not figured out how to live happily where they are—where, presumably, they must be.

I am ashamed to admit that at one time I succumbed to a bit of this self-pitying. I moved to Madison, Wisconsin, from Philadelphia. At the time, I thought Madison could never provide me with the thrills and luxuries of the hip, urban, sleek city I was leaving behind. I had made up my mind that no town a tenth the size of Philly, farther from Chicago than Philly was from New York, and twenty times as far from an ocean, could possibly be a suitable place to live. But the demand for philosophers is not what it was two thousand years ago, and so I was prepared to grit my teeth and suffer through life in what I felt was the third world.

Several things saved me from this fate. First: the friendships I made. Some of my new friends were also East Coast ex-pats who could empathize with my plight but also assure me that Madison had plenty to offer if I just gave it a chance. Other friends were Wisconsin natives whose obvious enjoyment of the state's offerings convinced me that there was more to Midwestern living than a quick glance could reveal. Second: my discovery that Madison is a city that provides innumerable rewarding trails for the eager runner—paths between lakes, through arboretums, through pastures, around a beautiful capitol building, and on and on. But most importantly, the positive outlook that Zen teaches showed me that it is a mistake to think that there are "bad" places to live. There are no bad places. If a spot on Earth seems intolerable, ask yourself why. You are in charge of whether the piece of ground that you call home is a place you can live happily, or a blight unfit for your continuing existence.

Selecting a Positive Route

This last lesson has an obvious application to runners who fault, for one reason or another, the running options open to them. There is no such thing as an inherently bad running route. If you dread all of your running options and can view the scenery moving past you only with distaste, this says more about you than it does the paths you have chosen.

That said, it is true that some running environments are easier to enjoy, and more conducive to setting your mind at peace, than others. Routes that put you in view of water, or through rolling countryside, seem to soothe the mind naturally and free it of negative emotion. On the other hand, running in a city is often fraught with incidents, mishaps, and frustrations that are likely to have the opposite effect on the mind. Likewise, if, for whatever reason, you find yourself unable to run outdoors and must take your workout on a treadmill or around a track, you might find yourself struggling against tedium—watching the clock and counting down the seconds until the run is over. Finally, the climate often makes even the most beautiful vistas hard to appreciate. The golden field through which you are running may not lift the spirits if the temperature is close to ninety-five and the humidity weighs on you like a wet beach towel. Likewise, the beauty of a sunrise can hardly be expected to fill your soul with a sense of well-being if your eyelashes are caked with frost and you have lost all sensation in your toes.

In short, although there may be no such thing as a bad running route, particular environments and conditions can make some runs *easier* to enjoy than others. In this chapter we'll look at how to make the most of the running options that are available to you. Because cities, treadmills, tracks, and harsh climates tend to be stingier with the pleasures they offer a runner, these will be my focus. By the chapter's end, you'll be prepared to find pleasure in whatever running environment you find yourself.

Running in the City

Because I lived in Philadelphia before moving to Madison, I know something about the difficulties that a runner in an urban environment faces. First there are the pedestrians who seem not at all interested in clearing a path for you as you try to maintain your pace down a sidewalk. These people act as if they have as much right to the sidewalk as you do even though they're not running! And it's not just people around you that you have to negotiate. There are baby strollers, shopping bags, wheelchairs, and, worst of all, umbrellas whose weather balloon diameters and dagger-tipped edges make them the scourge of rainy days.

And then, just when you think you've broken free from the crowd, having banged from one body to the next like a pinball, you're stopped dead in your tracks by a light that's just turned red. You now have thirty seconds or more to bide your time until the light changes in your favor. Do you stop your watch while you wait? Keep it going and jog in place? If you've stopped it, don't forget to turn it back on once you begin crossing the street. And watch out for that pothole! Don't trip over the curb once you get to the other side!

> **FROM THE MOUTHS** *of Runners*
>
> **ARIS 41, ALBANIA** "I live in a city where running is hard because of all the traffic and noise and people. It helps me to think of things just as things, rather than as good or bad. This way nothing bothers me."

Then there is the auto and bus traffic. If you're running during a busy time of day, which, in a major city, is about the only time of day that there is, even when you're lucky enough to hit an intersection while the light is green, this is no guarantee that you can make it safely across. There might be gridlock to contend with, or a bus that didn't quite make it through the yellow light might be sitting in your path like a beached whale, belching nasty fumes to enjoy while you wait for it to continue on its journey. Cars might be making right turns across your path. In some cities, it is legal to turn left on red if you're turning from a one-way street onto another one-way street. Better watch out!

If you have ever tried to run in a city, much of this probably sounds familiar. If you haven't, you might be wondering why anyone would bother. Well, believe it or not, a little Zen training can make urban running much less of an ordeal. In my case, by the time I left Philly, I had discovered how to take pleasure from *almost* every aspect of a city run. Notice that modifier *almost* . . . I should come clean. Even though I can and do run in a city, this takes some work. Developing and maintaining the frame of mind necessary to finish an urban run in anything but a state of frustration requires a kind of mental diligence that takes practice. Here we'll review the Zen skills you need to make the most of city running. It's up to you to practice them.

Running Through a City Mindfully

Let's go back to mindfulness and right effort. The first step in overcoming the irritation and distress that urban running so often produces is to analyze your own mind. You'll want to think very carefully about the emotions you experience as you try to run in a city and the causes of these emotions. Remember: the point of mindfulness is to develop a catalogue of exactly the emotions and attitudes that occupy your mind. Think of these emotions and attitudes as *tangible*—as objects with weight that can be detached from yourself. As we've discussed, Buddhists teach that attachments are the most basic reason for *dukkha*, or suffering, so you should seek to detach yourself from those items in your mind that do you harm.

Mindfulness, I have stressed, is not as easy as it may first appear. Most of us spend very little time studying our own minds. We might not realize that we're frustrated or angry or depressed until someone makes a comment like, "Don't snap at me; it's not my fault that the toast burned," or "Cheer up! It's a lovely day." Moreover, even on those occasions when we *are* aware that we are anxious or worried or sad, we often don't take the extra step to ask ourselves why we feel as we do. It's this extra step that Zen encourages us to take.

ZEN **Practice**

Imagine a running route that you know well. Try to visualize running it. Start with what you will see as you head down each straightaway, or as you turn each corner. Once you are able to "see" the route before you, add the sounds that you are likely to hear, and the odors you are likely to smell. Make the experience as real as you possibly can, and then ask yourself how you feel as you approach different parts of the run.

One way to uncover the reasons you don't enjoy city running is to think about what you feel *as* you run, and to try to identify why you are feeling what you do when negative emotions surface. However, this is probably not the best way to practice mindfulness, because, if you are doing it right, mindfulness demands serious concentration. In this case, you may be running along, concentrating so hard to sort out the attitudes and motives to which you have become attached, you run into a light pole, trip over a curb, or bang into a mailbox. If the accident itself doesn't kill you, the subsequent embarrassment might.

I think a better way to analyze your mind is to engage in the kind of virtual running I mentioned in the previous chapter. Close your eyes and imagine yourself running one of your typical routes through the city.

If you are preparing to run in a new city, of course you can't visualize your route, but cities are pretty much the same with respect to their obstacles to carefree running. On any one route you're likely to come across many of the same annoyances that you'd notice on any other. Where cities differ, I've discovered, is in the pleasures they offer.

You might find that even the thought of going on a *virtual* run begins to make you apprehensive. This, believe it or not, is a good sign. This means that your imagination is vivid and rich, and so it will be a more reliable guide to the goings-on in your mind as you actually run.

Separating What's Outside Your Mind from What's Within

Until you become more experienced with mindfulness, you are likely to attribute the causes of the negative emotions that you encounter to things going on *outside* your mind. This is understandable. You might think that you become frustrated when you run because of all the people on the sidewalk who get in your way, or because of the cars that fail to yield to pedestrians, or because of the light that seems always to turn red just as you reach the corner. The idea that your negative emotions are caused by events external to you is hard to give up. But, as appealing to common sense as this idea might seem, consider this. There are some people who love to run in cities. They love the bustle of the throng of people all trying to get where they need to go, the noise of car horns and ambulance sirens, the odors from hot-dog stands and chestnut vendors. These people have no special powers that you lack. They must still deal with the very same external events that anyone running through a city will come across. But then this shows that all the things you might hate about running in a city do not *have* to make you miserable. If they make you but not others miserable, then clearly *you* must have some role in this unhappy state of affairs. Annoyances are annoyances only if you let them be.

Without question, this point, which is central to Zen, is hard to accept. Common sense rails against the idea that our emotions and attitudes are at least as much of our own doing as they are the product of the outside world.

Because of the grip that common sense has on us, we must, in a sense, "sneak up" on the alternative Zen view. As you start your virtual run, forget for a moment the Zen lesson about your own role in the creation of negative emotions. Pretend, temporarily, that the frustrations you feel as you try to run through a city are in fact caused purely by things going on outside you. You might imagine leaving your house and having to walk over trash or broken glass to get to the corner where you'll start your run. These things, we are now supposing, cause you to feel resentment toward whoever left them there. You begin to run and have to avoid a mother pushing a baby carriage down the center of the sidewalk. You feel angry because she has taken you off your pace or caused you to miss a step. You get to the corner a second too late and must stop and wait a minute for the light to change. If it hadn't been for that woman with the baby carriage and this red light, you'd be on your way. The mother and the red light, or so it appears, are conspiring against you, thereby causing your present state of frustration. As you finally begin to cross the street, a car comes out of nowhere and honks at you as if you were at fault for heeding the walk sign. The close call leaves you frazzled.

Maybe you find your blood pressure rising just from reading this description. If you run in a city, this might sound familiar. If you haven't run in a city, this might have you thinking that you never will! But let's now approach matters from a Zen perspective. The first point to appreciate is that broken glass outside your door, obstacles on the sidewalk, red lights, and even close calls with automobiles are not in and of themselves sufficient reasons to become resentful, angry, frustrated, or frazzled. Indeed, this is hard to accept. But remember that the same external events that might fill you with negative emotions have the capacity to produce happiness or peacefulness in others. This shows that you are responsible for how the so-called irritations of city life affect your mental well-being.

Now that you have gone for a virtual run and have compiled a list of things that you typically blame for the unease that you feel as you *actually* run, you are ready to focus on the questions that will identify those features of your mind that are *really* to blame for your negative emotions.

Obstacle One: Litter

Resentment stirs in you when you find you need to walk over trash and broken glass that someone has thoughtlessly left outside your door. Without doubt, their action was thoughtless. You would not do such a thing, and why should you have to tolerate others doing such a thing to you? But, of course, no one has done this thing "to you." In acting thoughtlessly, they were not in any way out to insult *you*, or anyone else for that matter. A thoughtless act is just that—one taken without consequences in mind. Once you appreciate this, you can detach yourself from the idea that the trash on your stoop is some sort of attack on your person. Imagine simply wrapping the idea up in a brown paper bag and tossing it away (but not on your stoop with the other trash). Now one reason you felt resentment (presumed malice) each time you saw litter has disappeared.

Of course, you might still resent a person for behaving thoughtlessly, even once you understand that there was no malice intended. How, you might wonder, could people fail to see that dropping their refuse in front of your door is insensitive? Maybe they do realize it or maybe they don't. Either way, it does not really matter. What matters is how you respond to their thoughtlessness. We have already seen that it makes no sense to treat the litter as a personal attack. But responding to thoughtlessness with resentment or anger also makes no sense. The consequences of a thoughtless action do not go away if you choose to begrudge the perpetrator of the action. You can prove this to yourself. The next time someone does something thoughtless, become angry with the person and see whether this makes a difference to what he or she has done. I promise you that it will not. The only difference your agitation will make is to change your mood from something light to something dark.

You might even permit yourself to practice some right effort on this occasion. Remember, right effort is the Zen practice of replacing negative emotions or thoughts with positive ones. Instead of resenting someone for dropping trash in front of your house or apartment, you might be glad that they made the task of cleaning it up so easy. If you know that you are bothered by the ugliness of broken beer bottles or cheeseburger wrappers, you should be happy that some- one has dumped these things in a place where removing them is quick and convenient. Disposing of trash that's ten feet from your broom closet is far less work than disposing of trash that's fifty feet away, or a block away.

Obstacle Two: Pedestrians

The mother out for a stroll with her baby is not trying to get in your way. Chances are, if she realized you were charging up behind her she would try her best to step aside. If you think of the mother as someone who is intentionally set on disrupting your path, then it's no wonder that you feel angry that she has "forced" you to slow your pace or miss a step. You are attached to the idea that she has chosen this instant to take a walk just to thwart your desire to run. Or, perhaps you have attached yourself to the idea that sidewalks should be emptied of all pedestrians whenever you decide to go for a run. This is a nice idea. Perhaps the city churches can all ring their bells, or emergency warning sirens can be sounded, to indicate that sidewalks must now be cleared because you are ready to run. You get the point. Don't start your run with the idea that the sidewalks belong to you and that the people using them are nothing more than hazards you must avoid. Detach yourself from this thought and toss it aside.

There are times of the day when sidewalks are simply too con- gested to use for running. There is no Zen solution to this problem.

Zen can help you to focus your mind and rid yourself of negative emotions, but it can't make solid objects permeable. Zen can't make it possible for you to take up the very same space that someone else is already occupying. If you have to run at a busy time of day, you should make a point of confining your run to a park. Most large cities have parks that, if not large enough for a decent run, can at least provide space enough to run adequately sized laps. Another possibility is an outdoor track. If there is a university in your city that allows public access to its facilities, this would be a good place to try. You can also try running indoors if there are facilities available.

Obstacle Three: Traffic Lights

Streetlights turn red not to hinder you, but to regulate traffic. I realize that this does not mean that streetlights will *not* hinder you—of course they will. But if you detach yourself from the idea that the lights are somehow collaborating to disrupt your journey, you are far less likely to develop negative feelings in response to the hindrances that they occasionally impose. If the lights in your city are frequent and seemingly timed against runners, you might try this trick. Instead of attaching yourself to the idea that you must keep to a particular route, let the streetlights plan your route for you. Every time you reach a corner and are stopped by a red light, run with the green. If you are familiar with your city, you don't have to worry about becoming lost, and there is something liberating about leaving your route in the hands of fate (or the traffic planners). Indeed, there are parts of Philadelphia I probably would never have seen without letting the greens guide my way.

You should by now have an idea about how to approach urban running as a Zen runner. The issues of unsightly trash and unwieldy pedestrians apply in similar ways to the other obstacles you come across in a city.

Running Indoors

More than any other kind of running I dread running indoors: imprisoned in a room lit by flickering fluorescents, bound to smell the sweat of others' toils, condemned to listen to the incessant drone of fans, forced to exercise alongside gum-chewers, grunters, and jabberers. What could be worse? Okay. Perhaps I exaggerate the trauma that indoor running causes me when I let my Zen guard down. (If you have been paying attention, you'll realize that it is not running indoors that causes my trauma, but how I react to indoor conditions.) But, if I could, I would always run outdoors. What might possibly make me turn away from the outdoors and scurry, like a Punxsutawney Phil who has just seen his shadow, into a forsaken burrow? I can spell the answer with three letters: I-C-E. Every spring, as Wisconsin begins its thaw, there is a period where rain falls from the sky only to freeze on every surface that has the misfortune of being horizontal. Tree branches, cars, mailboxes, steps, sidewalks, streets, windowsills, power lines—all look like they've been lacquered with clear nail polish. If you fail to notice that all objects horizontal now have a high-gloss finish, then the first thing you'll do when you step out your door is fall on your butt. The second thing you'll do is try to stand up and then fall on your butt again. You can probably guess what the third, fourth, and fifth things to happen will be.

On days like these, running outdoors is simply impossible. Those doohickeys you can purchase that slip onto the soles of your sneakers and promise traction in icy conditions? Forget about it. These devices are worthwhile in some snowy and icy conditions, but not in conditions where the layer of ice is thin, smooth, hard, and covering pavement or cement. On days like these I usually won't run. But, if I'm desperate to get a run in, I'll crawl to the corner and catch a bus to the university where I can use facilities in the gym. The choice I have to make once I crawl from the bus stop to the gym is between running on an indoor track or running on a treadmill. This, for me, is a choice between a rock and a hard place.

RUNNING **Tip**

Indoor running does have a benefit. On those occasions when you find yourself on a track, take the opportunity to time how long it takes you to run a kilometer and a mile at your regular pace. This information can help you evaluate distances of unfamiliar routes, and it also lets you check your progress if you are training for a race.

Even if you don't dread running indoors as I do, if you have spent any time on a track you'll notice that it is wanting in certain respects. The scenery has all the interest of the background in an old Hanna-Barbera cartoon, repeating itself over and over again. Etiquette (and safety) requires that you always run in a single direction, which, after a few dozen laps, might cause some pain in your IT bands where they connect to your knee. You'll pass the same slower runners time and time again, and in turn be lapped by the same faster runners. In fact, you'll see in the next chapter that the constancy of indoor running provides a good opportunity for learning how to use running as a meditation exercise, and this is how I now approach all the indoor running that I do. Here, however, my goal is to offer some advice about how to make the most of running on an indoor track or, worse in my mind, on a treadmill. (Of course, everything I say here applies to running on outdoor tracks as well.)

Dealing with Monotony

Monotony is the terrible enemy the runner faces when confined to an indoor environment. Running takes a toll on the body, and without the distracting variation in scenery, altitude, direction, and temperature, the temptation to focus on the body's aches and pains becomes hard to resist. Monotony also invites boredom, which can all too often overcome a runner, creating a gap between the distance he or she had planned to run and the distance he or she actually runs. To stave off this monotony, many runners avail themselves of mp3 players. I do this too on occasion. Sometimes I'll choose music; other times I'll listen to books that I've downloaded. This works pretty well, but I've learned that I can't always count on my mp3 player. For one thing, after my house keys, my mp3 player could be the proud bearer of the "Most Forgotten Item" label. Other times, I'll remember my mp3 player but I will have forgotten to charge it. Then there are the occasions when one of my daughters has left the house without bothering to tell me that she's taken my mp3 player with her, providing me with the pleasure of a frenzied twenty-minute search for something that I could not possibly find. Finally, sometimes I simply don't feel like listening to music or books. I'd rather run unencumbered, even if this means having to find ways to combat the monotony of indoor running. Let's now see how Zen can help in this battle.

Running in the Moment

Zen teaches that all things are impermanent, and existence is limited to just the present moment. In one respect, this makes a good deal of sense. What's happened before is no longer with us. Nothing exists in the past. The past is simply a record of what existed during some present moment that is no longer. Similarly, the future has yet to be, and until it becomes the present, it contains things that only potentially but do not actually exist.

One way to make these ideas more tangible is to imagine that you are looking through a narrow window onto a busy one-way street. Your view of the cars, trucks, and buses is limited by the window's small width. The vehicles passing through your field of view are like objects that exist in the present moment. Once they leave your sight they are gone from view forever. And, as far as you can tell, no cars or buses exist until they enter your field of view. Only by moving in front of your narrow window do they become visible. These are like the future objects that exist only potentially. They do not become real until they enter the "window" of presence.

This way of looking at things makes the toil of monotony less burdensome. Why is this? Monotony is by its very nature an *extended* occurrence. Nothing can be monotonous for an instant. Monotony sets in only when the same sounds or sights repeat themselves over and over again. But, the insight we derive from the Zen perspective on permanence is that there is no such thing as the *same* sound or *same* sight repeating itself over and over again. What's happened before is gone, and what is yet to happen has not. There can be no monotony if at every present instant the world around us is completely new, novel, and unrepeatable.

This Zen way of looking at the world is no doubt hard to grasp at first. But hopefully it makes some sense to you in the abstract. The trick, of course, is to make it *work* for you. Try this. Next time you find yourself running indoors, set yourself the goal of taking one lap around the track, or spending one minute on a treadmill, while thinking about your experience from a Zen standpoint. Tell yourself that each step you take is a new step—the only step that now exists. Steps before are gone; steps to come are not yet. Each footfall has its own instant of existence. Focus on this. This is *running in the moment.*

Experience each step you take as if it were your first. Notice your surroundings. They are not what they were an instant ago and they will not be the same an instant from now. What are you seeing, hearing, feeling, smelling right *now*? And *now*? And *now*? Force yourself to let go of what you just experienced. That no longer exists. Don't try to anticipate what you will experience in a minute or even a second. That does not yet exist. Concentrate just on the contents of your mind in the instant that they appear.

I have suggested that you attempt to run in the moment for only one lap around the track or only one minute on a treadmill. I would bet that initially you are unable to run in the moment for even these short durations. You'll come to appreciate more fully in the next chapter just how difficult these first steps toward meditation really are. But, the good news is that even if your first attempts to run in the moment fail, you will find that the very challenge of trying to run in the moment, of trying to sustain the mindset according to which every present moment is new and distinct from all past and future moments, is often enough to break the monotony of indoor running.

A process appears monotonous only if you believe that the moment that just passed is here again for another visit. Zen denies that this is possible. Coming to terms with this insight takes some work. But whether you finally come to embrace the idea or instead find yourself struggling with it, I promise that your great efforts to run in the moment will help make indoor running less tedious for you.

Running in Severe Climates

Not all of us can live in Southern California, where a day that is not sunny and in the seventies is an aberration. In fact, not all of us would want to live where the climate is so consistent. I know I look forward to the changing climate that Wisconsin's four very different seasons bring. Southern California might be Eden for some, but not for me. To those of us who, by choice or not, live in areas that experience severe climates, Zen can offer assistance. These are the climates in which the mercury drops well below the zero mark or hovers around one hundred, or where the air is thick with humidity or dry as bone. Any of these conditions will make running a challenge. Zen training can prepare your mind to endure this challenge.

Using Zen in Harsh Conditions

What can Zen do to help you run through blazing heat or icy cold? Here is a Zen strategy that I've used with success. By now you should be familiar with mindfulness—the practice of taking a telescope to the items in your own mind. Next time you are running in extreme conditions, try this. Apply all your focus on what you are feeling in the moment. Imagine the feelings as objects, substances, things with dimensions and weight.

FROM THE MOUTHS *of Runners*

SCOTT 43, COLORADO "I've never regretted getting up and going for a run. But, I always regret it when I don't get my butt out of bed. In the winter, I tell myself that I only have to run fifteen minutes. I've never turned back after fifteen minutes, and I feel especially good after finishing a run that I thought would give me trouble."

For instance, suppose that you are rounding a lake and now find yourself running face first into breathtakingly cold wind. The cold air bangs into your face, freezing tears almost as quickly as they bloom from your eyes. Focus on the sensation of the wind against your face. Concentrate on what your tears feel like as they leak from your eyes and slither down your cheeks. Feel the frost crunching on your eyelids when you blink. The more intensely that you focus on what is happening in your mind, on what you are feeling and seeing and hearing, the easier it will be to imagine these sensations as material substances that you can separate from yourself. Doing this creates a distance between you and what you are feeling. Instead of being the subject *of* these feelings—of being, as it were, victim *to* them—you can treat them as items separate from yourself and available to your inspection.

ZEN **Practice**

Next time you run, concentrate on the feelings in your body. Try to experience each feeling one at a time, in isolation from the other feelings, so that your mind is full of nothing but that coldness on your cheeks, or that ache in your knee, or the sensation of the impact of your feet on the pavement. Try to imagine these feelings as having their own existence—as not being *your* feelings.

As you practice this, keep a catalog of the feelings and sensations that you are identifying. Create, as it were, a collection of these things. Say to yourself, "Here is a cold feeling on my forehead," "Here is a numbness in my toes," "Here is that sound of snow crunching under my feet," "Here is that warmth on my cheek as the tear glides across it," and so on. As you put yourself through this mindfulness exercise, you'll soon find that the feelings you are collecting seem no longer to be *your* feelings. The feelings have become disembodied. They are no longer attached to you, and you are free to inspect and observe them from a distance. Once this shift takes place—this shift away from being victim *to* these feelings and toward being an outside observer *of* these feelings—you will find your discomfort slowly dissipating, like steam rising from a cup of hot tea.

This same strategy works as well for running in very hot weather, although the inventory of sensations will, of course, differ.

Now you'll be focused on the heat you feel on the bottoms of your feet, the beads of perspiration you feel running down the center of your back, the tightness of the muscles around your eyes as you squint into the glare reflecting off the street, and so on. The more intensely you concentrate on these sensations, the easier it becomes to isolate them, confining them to a space outside yourself. Once you do this, you neutralize their effect on you. You render them harmless, or at least relegate them to mere irritants that present no real bother.

Incidentally, in addition to helping ward off discomforts that severe climates might cause, this kind of mindfulness can also be an effective means for noticing the first danger signs of hypo- and hyperthermia. Careful attention to every sensation you undergo will heighten your chance of detecting that you are shivering, or that your muscles are not responding in normal ways, or that you are no longer perspiring. Of course, there is no guarantee the illnesses to which severe climate makes you prone can be detected well enough in advance to prevent them. However, insofar as Zen mindfulness heightens your sense of self, you are more likely to notice warning signs of hypo- or hyperthermia when being mindful than when not.

In this chapter I have tried to show how Zen can help you make the most of your path even when it takes you through loud and busy cities, or round and round the same boring track, or into dangerous and inhospitable climates. Most of my suggestions will take practice. Remember, when you first began to run, you had to start with short distances at a slow pace until you had the stamina to go farther and faster. Training the mind is no different. I hope I have said enough to get you going, but *you* will have to put in the effort to make these techniques work. Fortunately, you're a runner. Putting in the effort is what you live for.

CHAPTER 4
THE MEDITATIVE RUNNER

By now you should have a pretty good sense of how Zen Buddhist principles can assist and facilitate your efforts to run. Whether you are having a hard time motivating yourself to run or preparing to run or tackling paths that are not optimal for running, Zen can be useful. You've seen that Zen concepts of mindfulness and right effort are important tools for recognizing, eliminating, and replacing the negative emotions that are so often the source of problems that runners confront.

Have you been able to give mindfulness and right effort an honest try? If so, chances are high that you have been pleased with the results. Ideally, you will have seen payoffs in your regular running routine. If getting yourself to a run had become a constant struggle, perhaps you are now able to motivate yourself with less effort. Perhaps you now have a better understanding of why you run and why your family might resent the time you spend running, and you have taken actions to relieve this tension. Hopefully you have turned formerly unpleasant running routes into tolerable, or even enjoyable, experiences.

But there is more to Zen running than this. So far, your application of mindfulness and right effort has been to the various nuts and bolts involved in running: making yourself run, making sure you are ready to run, and making the most of where you run. In this chapter, you'll learn how to transform your running into a meditative experience. Then you'll go one step further and explore how to gain complete awareness as you run.

Combining Running with Meditation

Why turn running into a form of meditation? Why seek awareness in the course of running? What benefits do these activities hold for a runner? Most immediately, Zen Buddhists practice meditation—indeed, the word *Zen* means *meditation*—because exercises like mindfulness and right effort are easier to perform when you have developed the mental discipline that meditation requires. Hence, learning to meditate will enable you to use mindfulness and right effort more effectively in the service of your running. But meditative running has other benefits—some intrinsic and others more of a pragmatic nature. Of intrinsic value is the tranquility and calm one can experience when engaged in meditative running. Many of us enjoying running because it helps to clear our mind of anxieties, or it leaves us feeling relaxed afterward. Meditative running amplifies these aspects of running, which makes your running experiences even more rewarding. In addition, running with awareness provides you with the opportunity to derive more pleasure from the paths you run, and it also puts you in better tune with events occurring in your body as you run.

On the more pragmatic side, as you'll see in following chapters, meditative running and running with awareness can soothe the kinds of disquiet that runners face when training hard, racing, or confronting challenges from injury or age. Learning to meditate while you run is not easy. Nor is entering a state of heightened awareness of the sort Zen Buddhists cherish. However, even if you are not completely successful in these endeavors, you will find that your running experiences become more meaningful and more pleasurable simply as a result of trying.

Preparing the Mind for Meditative Running

Those of you who are worried that meditation requires you to sit with your legs bent in a pretzel while uttering strange chants can now breathe a sigh of relief. Although the long-bearded yogi sitting on a mountain peak, legs bent beneath him, strange sounds emanating over and over from his mouth as he searches for the meaning of life has become the popular icon of meditation, this is not meditation as followers of Zen practice it. True, many Zen monks do sit in a lotus position while they meditate, but this is simply because they feel comfortable sitting this way for long periods. And, while some Buddhist schools do advocate the use of mantras to focus the mind, Zen meditation is silent. Finally, the search for the meaning of life is far from the goal of Zen meditation. Rather, the goal of Zen meditation is to empty the mind of all thoughts—good or bad—in order to reveal features of one's mind and one's world that would ordinarily go unnoticed. Zen meditation heightens awareness of your mind and your world.

Beginning Meditation

Before explaining how to integrate meditation into the activity of running, a few practice sessions without the complications that running adds to meditation will be very helpful. Here's how to begin.

1. Find a room where you can sit without interruption. This is as much to spare you from distractions as it is to save you from embarrassment, for reasons that will soon become clear. While you are meditating, you will want to focus on nothing but your breathing, so try not to sit in a busy or cluttered room. Otherwise, if books or CDs line the walls, in no time you'll find yourself reading titles, remembering plots or characters, forming melodies in your head, wondering how Bruce Springsteen and Buffalo Springfield got misfiled alphabetically, and so on. Similarly, if you are sitting behind a cluttered desk, you'll start to count the number of paper clips in the paper clip chain, or you'll wonder how many feet of tape are left on the roll, or you'll begin to speculate why scissors is plural, which will lead you to speculate about why pants is plural, and on and on. The bottom line: you want to find an environment where the task of focusing your mind will be as easy as possible.

2. Sit in whatever position you find comfortable, but not too comfortable. You should avoid plush couches and other pieces of furniture that present what I like to call "sleeping

hazards." As I grow older, I find that sleeping hazards have become much more common than they used to be.

3. Choose a spot on the wall in front of you on which to focus or, as I prefer, simply close your eyes. This step eliminates the potential distraction of objects that remain in the room.

4. Before you start trying to meditate, "listen" to what's going on in your mind. This helps you appreciate how the meditating mind differs from the undisciplined mind. In the undisciplined mind, a thousand thoughts might be going on at once: What should I make for dinner tonight? Boy, Pete really screwed up at work today. Glad it wasn't me. Boss came down hard on him. Like Ed Asner in the *Mary Tyler Moore Show*. I wonder what's on TV tonight? Can't stand those commercials—the ones for cleaning detergent. I really should scrub the sink. Maybe after dinner. What should I make for dinner tonight? And so on and so on and so on.

5. Begin to focus on your breathing. As you meditate, you will try to clear your mind of all those thoughts, just as you might clear off your cluttered desktop. In order to do this, you will need to divert your attention from the ramblings of your mind toward something else. Introductory guides to Zen meditation are nearly universal in their recommendation that Zen novices should begin their meditation exercises by focusing on their breathing. Concentrate on the sensation of breathing. As you inhale, feel the breath entering through your nose, cooling the back of your throat as it moves down your trachea, expanding your chest. Silently count "one." Now, as you count "two," feel your chest walls contracting as the air is pushed back up

your throat, warmer now, and out again through your nose. Concentrate all of your attention on inhaling and exhaling, counting inhalations with odd numbers and exhalations with successive even numbers until you reach ten. Then start over again. The point of beginning again at ten is to prevent the act of counting from becoming too onerous. You want to focus on your breathing—not on the counting.

When I first tried this exercise, I could not even make it through the first ten count without unwanted thoughts breaking through my concentration. I'd get to "four" or "five" and my attention would shift from my breathing to events that had happened earlier that day, or year, or decade; or it would move on to events that I was looking forward to that evening, or next year, or five years down the road. Keeping a noisy mind at bay is *hard*. It requires *tremendous* discipline, as you'll see for yourself when you try this exercise.

Labeling Unwanted Thoughts

When these unwelcome thoughts intrude into your concentration, do *not* try to wrestle them into submission. Your goal should be an uncluttered and tranquil mind, and this will be unobtainable if you are constantly struggling to suppress the thoughts and emotions that flit across your mindscape. Instead, the Zen response to these uninvited thoughts is to label them. Give them a name, so that if you care to return to them after meditating you can do so easily.

For instance, suppose that as you count your breaths, focusing on the sensations that each inhalation and exhalation produces, a thought about Valentine's Day bursts through your concentration.

It's only a week away and you have not yet made a dinner reservation. Don't dwell on this thought. Simply give it a label, like "Valentine's," and then let it go, returning again to your breathing.

You'll probably find that as you label your uninvited thoughts, letting them go becomes easier. Naming a thought makes it more solid or tangible, and thus gives it enough weight to allow you to "drop" it. The act of labeling, in effect, renders the thought inert so that you don't have to spend any more time with it.

ZEN **Practice**

Find a quiet spot to work on your meditation exercises. Choose a time of day when you are least likely to face distractions. If you don't feel too silly, you might even put a chair in a closet and practice there.

When I first started to meditate, I found that I could more easily prevent myself from following a particular thought if I named it aloud. (This was the other reason I suggested that you find a place to meditate where you wouldn't be interrupted!) As a thought about a class I was teaching zoomed in from left field, I would say out loud "intro course," and return my attention to my breathing. As my peace-seeking mind was bombarded with thoughts of what I needed to do to before heading out of town, I would announce to the walls "travel plans," and then resume the exhalation that I had momentarily suspended.

The reason to label intrusive thoughts is to render them harmless. You want to prevent them from upsetting the delicate focus you have aimed at your breathing. As I became better at labeling my thoughts instead of following them wherever they might lead, I no longer had to utter names for them out loud. I now label them internally, in the silent language of thought. You'll find also that as you train your mind to avoid the temptations and distractions that unwanted thoughts carry with them, these thoughts will slowly give up. Like a lover spurned too many times, they'll finally recognize that they are no longer wanted, and they'll leave you alone.

Working Your Way Up

When you first practice mediation, do so for only a minute or two. The difficulty of concentrating on nothing but your breathing will surprise you. Eventually, try to work your way up from two minutes to five minutes to ten minutes. If your meditation has been successful, you'll find that your mind has assumed an openness and attentiveness that—however transient—is, in a literal sense, *extra*ordinary. Why? Imagine that the undisciplined mind is like a chalkboard in Albert Einstein's office. Every inch of the chalkboard is covered with numerals, mathematical symbols, Greek letters, arrows, equations, and so on. If you stared at the chalkboard for ten minutes and then closed your eyes while I secretly added another numeral or symbol to the jumble, when you opened your eyes you probably wouldn't be able to find the addition. On the other hand, if you stared at a *clean* board for ten minutes and then closed your eyes while I drew a symbol on the board, when you opened your eyes you would probably notice the symbol immediately.

The undisciplined mind is like the cluttered chalkboard. Because it is full of changing and disorganized thoughts, all clamoring for attention, no single thought gets much notice. Meditation erases the mental chalkboard. Once the slate is clean, the thoughts that do appear can receive your full notice. This is the sense in which meditation enhances awareness.

Practicing Zen Running

Once you have practiced a bit with the breathing exercises and feel reasonably confident in your ability to label and disregard those thoughts that ordinarily occupy your mind, the time has come to take your meditation skills on a road trip. Meditating while running, or what I call Zen running, is an exhilarating experience. Like the so-called runner's high, unless you've experienced it, words can hardly do it justice. When successful, Zen running can bring you to a state of complete awareness of your body and your surroundings. While Zen running, you feel as if your body and the world into which you are advancing are a single whole.

Picking a Route

To start your Zen running, you will need to pick a route with which you are completely familiar. Ideally, it should not include distractions of the sort that urban runners typically face. I'm fortunate to live just a block from an arboretum that forms a perfect 10K route around a lake. I've run this route once or twice a week for about fifteen years now. I know it *better* than I know the back of my hand. Although it might be an exaggeration to say that I could run it blindfolded, it would not be *much* of an exaggeration. I avoid potholes, duck under low branches, and hop the muddy spots without having to think about it. If you have no route of which you can boast this kind of familiarity, Zen running will be more difficult for you—but not impossible. Alternatively, you might initially want to try Zen running on a track or a treadmill, where the path ahead of you holds no surprises.

Trying Meditation on the Move

Once you've selected your route, begin your run as you usually would. I always find that my body requires at least half a mile to fall into an easy cadence, at which time any aches or kinks disappear. The more experienced a runner you are, the quicker you will find this rhythm, although I should confess that on some occasions I'll finish a run without ever finding an easy pace. Still, in general, once your body has become accustomed to running, it finds a posture and speed that just seem natural.

BUDDHA **Says**

You will not be punished for your anger. You will be punished by your anger.

Having hit your stride, the time has come to try your hand at *meditation on the move*, as it were.

1. To begin, keep your gaze fixed on the road at a point about fifteen feet ahead of you. This can be dangerous if you don't know what's coming, and this is part of the reason to attempt Zen running on a very familiar path. Continue for about half a mile until you feel comfortable doing this.
2. Start counting steps. Every time your left foot hits the ground, give it a count. Continue this until you reach ten, and then

start again. Don't try to count both left and right steps; you would need to count too quickly, which in itself can be a source of distraction.

3. Focus on each instance of your left foot hitting the ground. Strive to reach the same level of focus that you gave to each breath in your earlier meditation exercises. Feel the impact of your foot on the surface: the way the heel fits first, followed by the ball, which expands under the pressure of your body's weight. Feel your toes as they bend into the step, and spring your foot into the air behind you.

4. Label and release intruding thoughts. As before, it will be difficult to maintain your concentration on the feeling of each step to the exclusion of those other thoughts that scream for your attention. But, if you have already developed some skill in meditation, you can handle these undesirable intruders. You know what to do. Attach labels to them. Toss them aside with the knowledge that you can deal with them at a later time. Clean your mind. Erase its contents.

5. Continue to hone your awareness so that the only thoughts present are those of your feet hitting the surface beneath you and that spot on the road fifteen feet ahead of you. If you've done this right, you'll no longer notice, for example, that your feet are cold. That thought about cold feet will have been labeled and dropped overboard.

6. Don't let yourself become frustrated. Maybe after a minute of Zen running, the thought about cold feet returns to haunt you. Don't allow this to frustrate you. Frustration will only add to the number of thoughts and emotions that are trying

to force their way back onto the clean chalkboard of your mind. Instead, allow the thought some space on the chalkboard. There it is. You've noticed it. Now erase it.

7. Keep practicing. Follow this procedure for other thoughts and emotions as they emerge from your subconscious and vie for your attention. As with your previous efforts at meditation, you'll find that after a while you have become more proficient at taming these unwanted thoughts, and in time they'll no longer try so hard to interrupt the tranquility that you have achieved.

During Zen running, as you count your steps, gently noticing and erasing whatever thoughts become visible on your mental chalkboard, you'll find that you gradually lose sense of your body's efforts. I have a hunch that experienced runners know what I'm talking about even if they have never made a conscious effort to meditate.

ZEN **Practice**

Once a week, try to insert a few minutes of meditation into your running. After you get into this habit, you can try extending the period of meditation by a few more minutes, or meditating during two runs per week. Don't be discouraged if you are unable to develop this skill right away. It's tough, but with practice, you'll get it.

The difference between experienced runners and novices is doubtless in part a difference in physical conditioning, but it is also a difference in *attitude*. Novices have not yet learned how to push aside thoughts about what their bodies are doing when they run. All of their mental energy is focused on that stitch in their side, or that ache on the outside of their knee, or that blister on the end of their toe. It's no wonder that so many people who begin a running regimen with the noblest intentions end up burning their shoes after just a week. The discouragement these beginners suffer is due less to poor physical conditioning than it is to an inability to take control over the negative thoughts that plague them with each stride.

The steps toward Zen running I have recommended will help put you in charge of the thoughts that occur to you while you run. Those cramps, aches, and blisters that trouble novice runners, making each step feel like the hardest thing they have ever done in life, don't *demand* your attention. You're the boss. If you don't want to pay them attention, you don't have to. Zen runners understand this. The reason to introduce meditation into your running routine is to help you achieve the sort of mastery of mind that puts you in control of what you notice as you run. As we will see in future chapters, this ability comes in very handy when you are training, racing, or dealing with injuries.

Running with Zen Awareness

There's a flip side to Zen running that brings with it a special pleasure. Recall that the goal of Zen running is to use meditation techniques to empty your mind of all thoughts. Cleared of thought, your mind is like the smooth surface of polished marble. All the thoughts that might ordinarily trouble you—thoughts about work, family, and so on—are temporarily dormant. Those aches and pains that sometimes accompany you on your run have slid off the slick marble surface of your mind. This is what Zen running is about.

But, once you have attained this state of Zen running, you are in a position to enjoy a special kind of awareness, or what we'll call *Zen awareness*. I already mentioned this sort of awareness when I introduced the chalkboard metaphor in the earlier part of this chapter. A chalk stroke on a board that is already covered with chalk strokes is unlikely to be noticed. You simply cannot detect the new stroke amidst the confusion created by all the old strokes. Minds can be cluttered in the same way. I'm sure you have experienced this. There is simply too much happening in our lives not to fall victim to mental clutter. While thinking about an article I am writing, thoughts about my daughter's concert that evening might pop into my head, interrupted by thoughts about the leak in the roof, displaced by my realization that I need to buy cat litter on the way home from work, knocked aside by the memory that the car is low on gas, and so on. With all these thoughts scrambling and clawing for my attention, no one of them can possibly receive more than passing notice.

Meditation wipes the board clean. It sweeps away the clutter. And now we are in a position to understand how meditation can enhance your awareness. Just as a single chalk stroke on an otherwise clean chalkboard is immediately and completely conspicuous, so a single thought, sensation, or emotion in an otherwise empty mind can be an object of your full, undivided attention. In this way, meditation makes *full* awareness of these things possible, which can add a new dimension of pleasure to your runs. I will explain this in more detail shortly.

Beginning Awareness Training

For now, however, let's go back to the beginning. Return to that room where you initially practiced your breathing exercises. This time, bring along an object such as a flower, an egg, or even just a coin. This object is soon to be the focus of your *undivided* attention.

Place the object on a desk or table in front of you. If there is no surface available, just keep the object in the palm of your hand. Now I want you to begin your meditation, except instead of closing your eyes or focusing on a point on the wall, keep your eyes trained on the object. Begin to count your breathing, and don't let the object distract you. Your goal, as before, is to empty your mind, but now you do not want to empty it completely. Rather, you want to leave just *one* thing in your mind—your perception or awareness of the object before your eyes.

You might actually find meditation easier with an object on which to focus. As you concentrate on the thing in front of you, you might find that your ability to block out other thoughts grows stronger. If so, that is fine. Meditation for Zen Buddhists is about an end state. The means to this state are of little consequence if they get you where you should be going.

As unwanted thoughts begin to drift into your mind, label them as before, and then let them fade from view. You'll feel your mind quieting. This time, don't try to achieve a state of emptiness. Instead, continue to focus your gaze and allow the object to fill your mind. If you are doing this correctly, you'll notice that your current awareness of the object differs from your usual awareness of the object. This is because our usual awareness is influenced by our previous experience. For example, if your partner brought you roses on your first date, you may love roses. But if you've been pricked by thorns in your garden, you may dislike them. In essence, our previous experiences *bias* our conceptions of the world, so that we can't help but perceive things in light of these past experiences.

BUDDHA **Says**

We are shaped by our thoughts. We become what we think.

The example of the rose is, of course, none too subtle. However, you don't have to be scratched by a thorn to think negatively about a rose. Perhaps, with no conscious awareness of doing so, you associate roses with funerals. This will make some difference in how you perceive roses on future occasions. The more general point is that our perceptions of the world, of each other, and even of our own selves, are prejudiced in a way. They carry the marks of our previous experiences, forcing us to see things in a positive or negative light.

In contrast, when we perceive the world through the lens of meditation, we are perceiving it as it *actually* is. That negative emotion you experience when you see a rose is not because of anything the *rose* does. Rather, the rose appears to you in a negative way because of the thoughts, associations, and memories that you attach to it. Because meditation gets rid of these thoughts, associations, and memories, you are now in a position to see the rose as it really is—perhaps for the very first time. Your awareness of the rose before meditation was an awareness filtered through your beliefs and emotions; your awareness of the rose during meditation is unfiltered. You are finally just seeing the rose. You'll see red petals, but now they'll no longer be *blood* red; they'll simply be red. Those nasty looking thorns will no longer appear nasty looking. They'll be just thorns. This is what it means to have Zen awareness of the world.

Trying Awareness on the Move

Now it's time to take these tips for attaining Zen awareness out for a ride. Plan a run on the same path where you have been practicing your Zen running. After going through your warm-up, start to count your left footsteps. If you've done this several times already, then you should feel yourself readily falling into a Zen frame of mind. This time, however, instead of striving to empty your mind, choose something to fill your mind. If you're running through wooded paths, as I do, take your eyes off the spot fifteen feet in front of you and let them fall instead on the leaves of the trees. Allow nothing but your perception of the leaves into your consciousness. Try to see them as they really are rather than as they appear through the filter of your beliefs, desires, emotions, and biases. Give the leaves your full attention. Notice their patterns of colors, the dark round bruises that appear on their surfaces, the serration of their edges, the veins that run like rivers through them. There is no *you* separate from the leaves—there are just leaves.

If you are running through a light drizzle, empty your mind of everything except the sensations that the raindrops cause on your skin. Feel the cool touch of the drops as they hit your cheeks.

Feel the weight of the drops on your shoulders. Notice how the drops run the length of your nose and hang on its tip for just a second before letting go and falling to the ground. Many people will use rain as an excuse not to run, but this shows only that they have never developed a Zen awareness of rain. Those drops falling from the sky are not a reason to cancel a run. Full awareness of these drops—perceiving them as they really are—shows them to be neither good nor bad. They are what they are: cool, round beads of water. That's all they are; that's all Zen awareness shows them to be.

BUDDHA **Says**
The foot feels the foot when it feels the ground.

You might also choose to make your own body an object of Zen awareness. I find this useful to do especially when I'm recovering from an injury and am worried about reinjuring myself. If, for instance, I've just recovered from *plantar fasciitis*, I'll make myself fully aware of the sensations in my heel and along the arch of my foot as I run. Now I have a clearer idea of the severity of the injury and the care it requires. I've known people who routinely reinjure themselves because they tell themselves that the pain they feel is not really there, or not really significant. This is a clear example of perceiving through a filter of beliefs and desires—of failing to perceive things as they really are. Similarly, some people are so worried about aggravating an old injury that they become *too* sensitive to the smallest twinges. Instead of seeing these twinges for what they really are—inconsequential pangs that are gone almost as soon as they appear—they allow their concerns and worries to transform these little pains into life-threatening wounds!

Making Meditation and Awareness a Regular Part of Your Runs

The lessons presented here are not easy to learn. I know some people who have given meditation an honest go, only to discover that they are unable to do it. While Buddhists believe that we all have a Buddha nature—that we all are capable of enlightenment to some degree or other—some who attempt the meditation and awareness exercises described here will not succeed, or will succeed only modestly. This is okay. None of the practical Zen advice from the previous chapters, which deal with motivation and preparation, requires an ability to meditate. However, even if meditation seems to elude your best attempts, and even if the descriptions of Zen awareness leave you cold, the benefits that meditation and awareness can bring to your running make them worth your continuing effort.

If, for instance, you have tried several times without success to empty your mind of all but the sensations of breathing, don't let this prevent you from trying to meditate while running. As I noted before, breathing and counting are the customary tools for Zen meditation only because they have proved successful for many people. This is not to say that they will work for everyone. Perhaps if you are an experienced runner and find sitting still a chore, you will discover that you have less trouble meditating while you run than you do when you struggle to keep yourself confined in a chair. So, if the traditional means to empty your mind fail, don't be discouraged. You might find some other way.

Similarly, if you are able to empty your mind but for only a minute or two, or if you find that you cannot empty your mind completely but are able to calm your mind through some effort, recognize that this is a great start. None of us, or at most very few of us, were able to run 10K the first time we tried running. As a runner, you know the importance of starting small and building up. Meditation is no different. You need to set your sights on small goals at first. This means putting aside just a minute or two a day, or every few days, to meditate. There's no need to rush the process. Let your meditation skills develop at their own pace. If you become frustrated while you strive to meditate, stop. Give it another try some other time. Frustration will only make your task more difficult. If your attempts to meditate have all been at the same time of day or in the same environment, try changing these variables. You might discover that you're too hungry early in the morning to free your mind from the desire to eat, or too tired in the evening to approach meditation with the concentration that it requires. Perhaps the trees waving their branches outside the window are distracting you, or maybe the drone of the refrigerator in the next room is gnawing at the edges of your consciousness. At a new time, in a new place, your efforts to meditate might meet with a happier end.

Practicing Awareness

Zen awareness, too, can be elusive even after having succeeded to some degree in meditation. We've become so entrenched in our views about how the world is and should be that we often need to struggle heroically to see the world from a neutral perspective. As with meditation, you might find that your attempts at Zen awareness meet with only limited success at first. If so, practice Zen awareness using items for which you *know* you have some kind of bias. This is how I learned to distinguish how things seem to me, through the filter of my own mind, from how things really are. The item I chose was something I have loathed since a horrid experience at an early age: mayonnaise.

I needn't bore you with the details of this nasty experience. I'll say just that it culminated in vomit. Lots of it. All mine. Since that day, I had not been able to look at mayonnaise without seeing it as disgusting. Its texture seemed revolting; its color pallid; its aroma nauseating. You get the picture. I didn't like the stuff.

Curiously, I had none of these reactions to sour cream, yogurt, or vanilla pudding, any one of which might be cast as a very successful understudy to mayonnaise. Clearly my reaction to mayonnaise was a product of the attitudes my perceptions filtered through. This is why mayonnaise was a good choice for me to use when I began to practice Zen awareness. I asked my wife to place of dollop of mayonnaise in a bowl on the desk in my study (I didn't even want to open the jar). I then meditated for a while, clearing my mind as best I could of thoughts, emotions, opinions, and so on. Next I allowed my attention, unsullied by all the anxieties and emotions that make my encounters with mayonnaise ordinarily so disagreeable, to wander to the mayonnaise, trying to see the mayonnaise for what it really is.

I admit that my first trials were not easy going. It took several such efforts before I could witness the mayonnaise without feeling queasy. But, over time, my perception of the mayonnaise truly changed. I was able to see it simply for what it is: a whitish shiny glob with a slight yellow tinge. That's all mayonnaise is when viewed from the vantage of a mind emptied of its prejudices and fears.

Of course, I still hate mayonnaise, and unless I've prepared myself for its presentation, its sight still leaves a bad taste in my mouth. This shows only that Zen works! The awareness of mayonnaise that I attain through Zen is completely distinct from my ordinary awareness of mayonnaise.

I hope this example helps you understand what Zen awareness is and how you might know when you've attained it. I firmly believe that your running will benefit from both Zen running and Zen awareness. If you are able to work both activities into your regular running routine, you will be more relaxed during your runs, and you will complete your runs feeling more refreshed than usual. You'll also find that the time you spend running will go by more quickly. Indeed, depending on how adept you become at these skills, you may be surprised to find yourself at the end of your run without having any memory of the steps that took you there. This is because as you meditate or practice awareness, you cannot also think about how much farther you have to go, how steep that hill up ahead is, how wet or heavy your feet are, and so on. Or, if you choose to be aware of these things—aware in the Zen sense—you will not be bothered by them. You will see them as they really are, uninfected by the negative attitudes you might otherwise attach to them.

Recognizing the Limitations of Meditation and Awareness

Although this all sounds pretty good, I am not interested in selling snake oil. Meditation and awareness are not panaceas for all troubles that a runner might encounter. In fact, I don't often try to meditate or achieve awareness during my normal running routine. I like to run, whether meditating or not, whether striving for awareness or not. But I do think that Zen running and Zen awareness have an important role to play when engaged in certain kinds of running. Zen tools make training more tolerable, racing more enjoyable, and accepting injuries and the effects of aging more bearable. We'll look at each of these issues in the chapters that follow.

CHAPTER 5
TRAINING THE ZEN WAY

These days, or so it seems, for every good cause there is a race. In my hometown, hardly a week goes by when there isn't an organized race to benefit nurses, firefighters, teachers, the homeless, literacy, AIDS or cancer patients, and so on. These are all worthy causes, and I am happy to spend money both to contribute to the relief efforts and to enhance the fulfillment that I usually feel after running ten kilometers. As well, long-distance runs that aren't related to a cause have become very popular in recent years. For instance, in Madison alone there is an annual 20K race around one of our lakes, a twenty-mile race to celebrate Norwegian independence day, a marathon, a half marathon, and an Ironman (an endurance triathlon that culminates with a marathon). Within a three-hour drive, there are marathons and half marathons in Chicago, Milwaukee, the Fox Cities, Green Bay, and probably other places I don't even know about. If you live in a city, you can probably relate. But regardless of where you live, a few minutes on the Internet will reveal numerous races, at all times of the year, within a few hours' driving distance from your home. Obviously, the twenty-first century is a good one for runners!

RUNNING **Tip**

To find an organized run near you, check out *www.active.com /running*. Just enter a location in the search window and you'll find links to nearby running events. You can use this site not just to find races near your home, but also to see whether any of your travels might be combined with a running event.

Whether you've been running for a while, or whether you're a novice who has been cajoled, compelled, or coerced into running a race in support of the favorite cause of your spouse, boss, or parent, you'll need to train to do it right. If you've never run, you cannot wake up on race day and hope to complete a distance of 10K, or, probably, even 5K. Similarly, if your longest distances have been 10K, you can't possibly complete a marathon without further training.

A student in one of my classes once told me he was going to run a marathon the following weekend. He was eighteen and very fit from the soccer practices he'd been attending all semester. I asked him what his longest run had been to date and he told me it was ten miles. I held my tongue. Maybe he could do it? Eighteen-year-old bodies are capable of much more than forty-eight-year-old bodies, after all. The Monday following the marathon, there was no sign of him. On Wednesday he came limping into the classroom, *still* sore from the twenty miles of the marathon that he was able to run. To his credit, he finished the race, walking the final six miles. "Tougher than I thought it would be," he mumbled after the lecture.

This chapter and the next focus on how to train the Zen way for various races in your future, and how, once the starting gun sounds, you can perform at peak efficiency during your trip to the finish line. Zen can't promise you medals and heavy winners' purses, but most runners who race don't do it to win. We race for the sake of helping some cause, or for the camaraderie, or, probably most often, for the additional challenge and feelings of satisfaction that races add to our regular running routines. If you've ever participated in a race, you know the extra exhilaration it brings to a run. If you haven't, you should. Racing is a first-try addiction, but unlike other first-try addictions, it's relatively inexpensive, good for your health, and won't land you in jail. In this chapter you'll learn how Zen can help you through the training that is necessary to prepare for a race. The next chapter focuses on how Zen can be of service during the race itself.

Understanding the Philosophy Behind Different Training Programs

There is no such thing as the right way to train, because people respond differently to different training programs. Some runners read about the training programs that professional marathoners put themselves through and decide that they ought to be doing the same thing, believing what works for the best should work for the rest. This theory is completely wrong, and it nearly always leads to the path of injury. Most important when training is that you find a regimen that works for you—that leads you to your goal with a minimum risk of injury.

Perhaps because people differ so much with respect to their natural abilities, their base levels of fitness, their nutrition, and the time they can afford to exercise, there are a variety of different training philosophies, each with an avid league of followers. However, use caution when you hear runners sing the praises of a training routine that decreased their 10K time by four minutes, or increased their distance from 10K to 20K in only two weeks, or brought them close to breaking the sound barrier. There's no reason to suspect that these runners are trying to mislead you, but you shouldn't expect that just because a particular training program worked wonders for Scott or Ann it will work for you as well.

For example, I remember the first time a member of my running group told me about the speed work he'd been doing on a local track. He'd brought his 5K time down by three minutes. "I gotta try that!" I thought. I did, and I spent the next two weeks recovering from a pulled calf muscle. My next 5K event was two minutes slower than the one I had done before adopting my friend's training program.

Which training program is for you? This is impossible to say; you should try out several, starting cautiously before devoting your full commitment to the one that seems to work best for you. Hopefully, that way you won't end up hurting yourself as I did. In the next section, I'll describe a few different training philosophies, and then show you how to apply Zen to make your choice work best for you.

Pacing Runs

Pacing runs are used primarily to build speed. The idea with a pacing run is that you *slowly* build from your present ability to the distance and speed that you'd like to run. For instance, if you are already running 10Ks but want to improve your time, increase your pace to the speed you desire for a single mile of your ordinary run. Don't choose the first mile of your run as the one to complete faster. Use the first mile to warm up, and then increase your speed for the second or third mile. Once you're comfortable with the quicker pace, adopt the same pace for another mile of your 10K, sandwiching a mile at your old pace between them. Eventually, you'll be able to run all 10K at the quicker pace. This method is sometimes called *pacing training*, because you never try to run faster than the pace that you want to maintain during a race.

Speed (or Interval) Training

There are several ways to go about speed, or interval, training. The basic idea is that you run *faster* than the pace at which you hope to race in order to make it easier for you to run the pace you desire *during* the race. You can incorporate speed intervals into your ordinary runs, choosing to run two hundred meters or more at the quick speed and then returning to your normal pace for a mile before picking up the pace again. Or, you might try replacing an ordinary run with focused speed work, where you run a speed interval, recover for a short period, repeat the interval again, recover, and so on. This second approach to speed work must be done with special care to prevent injury. If you try it, be sure to warm up adequately with a mile of jogging before you get down to business. It's best also to cool down with another period of jogging after you finish with the speed work.

Hill Training

The philosophy behind hill training is the same as the one behind speed training. You are trying to increase your stamina by pushing your body to its limit, with the expectation that you will then have an easier time marginally increasing your regular distance or speed. As with speed work, you have the choice of incorporating hills into your ordinary runs, or devoting a session or two a week just to hill training. If you choose the second option, you can use the hill itself to fix your recovery time between climbs. Run up the hill at a fast pace, and then slowly descend while you catch your breath. Once down, up you go again, and so on. Of course, not everyone has the option of doing hill work. If you live on the salt flats of Utah, for instance, you'll search far and wide before you find anything worth climbing.

Low-Distance Training

The philosophy behind low-distance training is that *how* you spend your time training is more important than spending a *long* time training. Rather than incorporating speed or hill intervals into your weekly running, or dedicating one or two days of the week to them, low-distance training makes these exercises the focal point of your routine. A typical week of low-distance training might include one day devoted to your usual run, while other days of the week are dedicated to speed work, hill climbing, and running at your racing pace. Because the goal of low-distance running is to make the most of the time you spend running, this can be a good program for people who are too busy to set aside long hours for training. On the other hand, this is the kind of training that can sap the joy out of running. It's like reading Cliffs Notes rather than enjoying the pleasures of the novel itself.

Long-Distance Training

At the opposite end of the spectrum from low-distance training is long-distance training, or what some call *slow training*. This is the most time-consuming form of training, but it is also the gentlest of the programs listed here. It's simple: you gradually add miles to your weekly gross, keeping the same pace that you ordinarily use. Long-distance training is the method I prefer when preparing for marathons. If my typical Sunday run, usually the longest of my week, is between six and ten miles, I'll start adding distance to it. Similarly, if my mid-week runs are usually around five miles, I'll bump them up a bit too. Over a matter of weeks my Sunday runs will grow closer and closer to a marathon distance, and the mid-week runs will also grow, but never beyond seven to ten miles.

Not only will long-distance training improve your endurance, it will also increase your speed on those shorter runs. If you can run fifteen or twenty miles at an eight-minute pace, you should be able to race a 10K event at a seven-minute pace with no problem.

Naturally, long-distance training is not for those pressed for time. If you are training during a time of year that is especially cold or unbearably humid, this is also probably not the regimen for you. I like to run the Mad-City Marathon in my hometown, which takes place on

Memorial Day weekend, and this means that I long-distance train during the spring. This is a beautiful time of year in Madison. The snow finally melts, buds appear on the trees, and crocuses pop from the ground like champagne corks. When better to log those long miles?

Taking Care When You Train

Before delving into how Zen can help with your training routine of choice, a word of caution is in order. You should not attempt any of these training methods except, perhaps, long-distance training until your base level of fitness is such that you can run 5K comfortably. At a comfortable level, you should be able to converse freely as you run. (Talking to yourself does not count!) Also, if at any time while training you feel sharp pains in your muscles or joints, or pain in your chest, stop immediately. This may put you behind schedule, but if you injure yourself or die from a heart attack you'll be even further behind. Finally, don't attempt to train every day of the week. Training is hard work and your body needs time to recover and rest. When you begin training, three or four days per week is enough. Eventually you'll increase this to five or six days. Always be sure to allow at least one day of the week for resting and recuperating.

Training with the Buddha: The Middle Way to Train

We've already seen that Buddhism has a lot to say about disciplining the mind. A disciplined mind—a mind fully aware of itself and capable of casting aside unwanted negative thoughts and feelings— can be the runner's greatest asset. We've also seen how Zen running, running in the moment, can keep the runner's mind at peace. Zen runners have an enhanced awareness of their bodies and their surroundings. But there is still more to learn from Zen. Of central importance to the Buddha's dharma, or teachings, is the idea of The Middle Way. The Middle Way should be the keystone of any training program.

Considering Siddhartha and The Middle Way

The Buddha's discovery of The Middle Way is an interesting story in its own right. About 2,500 years ago, the prince Siddhartha, who was to become the Buddha, lived a pampered life in his father's palace in northern India. Siddhartha's father did everything within his power to prevent the young prince from learning about misfortune and suffering. Within the palace walls the king ensured that young Siddhartha was never exposed to death or aging or illness. Even the flowers in the palace gardens were replaced before they withered. Siddhartha's life was one long feast, accompanied by musical entertainment and the attentions of beautiful women. On those occasions when Siddhartha ventured forth from the palace, his father would make sure that all signs of unhappiness, poverty, and disease were swept clean from the paths Siddhartha would follow.

BUDDHA **Says**

To live a pure unselfish life, one must not count anything as one's own in the midst of abundance.

Of course, things could not go on this way forever. Eventually, Siddhartha must have guessed that all was not as it seemed. So at twenty-nine, Siddhartha crept unnoticed and disguised from his home on four consecutive nights, taking with him only a servant as his guide. During these outings, Siddhartha learned of the suffering that all normal human beings experience in the course of a lifetime: illness, aging, death, sorrow. But Siddhartha also came across a monk with a begging bowl who, the servant explained, had given up all his possessions and had dedicated his life to searching for the meaning behind all this suffering.

Perhaps inspired by the monk's mission, Siddhartha spent his next six years on a similar quest. He wandered the country. He spoke to teachers and mystics. He starved himself, reducing his diet to a single grain of rice each day. Legend has it that he became so thin it was possible to touch his backbone through his stomach. Finally, at the age of thirty-five, Siddhartha realized that his asceticism was taking him no closer to the truth. He began to eat again. He gained strength. Still determined to find answers to questions about the meaning of life and the point of suffering, Siddhartha decided to sit beneath the Bodhi Tree (as it came to be called) until he saw the truth. Following a night of intense meditation, Siddhartha became the Buddha, the enlightened one. He spent the remainder of his life, another forty-five years, teaching others how they too could find enlightenment.

Grasping the Lesson of The Middle Way

Buddhism's Middle Way is easy to grasp. It's something we all know intuitively, but that runners especially tend to ignore. As a young man living a life full of indulgences, the Buddha was unaware of the world around him. He had no idea of the realities, many of them harsh, that his fellow human beings faced in their ordinary lives. All he knew was pleasure. The Buddha went from this extreme to another. While walking the country looking for enlightenment, Siddhartha starved himself. His life was one of deprivation and suffering. Despite this radical change, from spoiled child to starving monk, the Buddha was still no closer to understanding the big questions in life. Not until the Buddha began to eat again and to regain the strength that had left his broken body did he find enlightenment.

The lesson here is that extremes in life should be avoided. The Middle Way is the road to follow, not because it is easier or safer or requires less effort, but because our bodies and minds perform at their best when they are not operating in extreme conditions. The Buddha had spent six years searching for enlightenment, but, on reflection, consider how distracted from his goal he must have been as his body constantly craved nourishment. How could he concentrate on the BIG issues when his mind was probably wandering to thoughts of succulent fruit, goblets of wine, and honeyed sweets? On the other hand, when he lived in his father's palace, the opiates of pleasure prevented young Siddhartha from entertaining the idea that there might be more to life than beauty, food, and gracious company. Obviously, neither lifestyle was conducive to deep thought. Thinking clearly—thinking at peak efficiency—required a life *between* the extremes.

This idea that The Middle Way is the best way, in the sense that it is the way that provides our minds and bodies with something like the most favorable operating conditions, is a familiar one. If you're a reflective person, I doubt you are surprised by this. Nevertheless, it's a message that some find very hard to incorporate into their daily lives. For instance, most of my colleagues are workaholics. They get up in the morning before the sun rises and work steadily until late in the evening—taking breaks only for more coffee and enough food to keep their stomachs from grumbling. I often wonder whether the long hours my colleagues spend working actually diminish their productivity. On the other hand, I also know people, fortunately none with whom I work, who complain about having to get out of bed in the morning—as if the very act of living is almost too much to bear. They move through the day finding excuses not to work, cutting corners at every opportunity, always on the lookout for an opportunity to push their duties onto others. Obviously, neither of these lifestyles—the workaholic's nor the sloth's—is sustainable. Workaholics will burn out. Sloths will lose their jobs. Both kinds of people need to move toward a life in which their work is integrated more appropriately into life's other activities. Runners need to take very seriously the importance of The Middle Way. This is especially true when training.

Looking for The Middle Pace

Pace training, remember, requires that you add intervals at racing pace to your regular runs. The idea is to acclimate your body to the pace you hope to *maintain* during the actual race. The concept of maintenance is crucial. If the pace you set your sights on is too fast, you will not be able to maintain it for the duration of a race. More likely, you'll burn out well before the race's end, crawling through the finishers' chute and vowing never to race again.

On the other hand, you never want to finish a race feeling like you could run another mile, or even another ten feet. If you've done your pace training correctly, you'll have spent all your energy during the actual race. There should be no leftovers. The trick, of course, is to find The Middle Pace—a pace that allows you to finish the race, but just *barely*.

Discovery of The Middle Pace is often a matter of trial and error. When you begin pace training, choose one or two days of the week to insert half a mile of quicker pace into the middle of a 5K run, or a full mile of quicker pace into the middle of a 10K run. Try to run this interval five to ten seconds faster than your ordinary pace. This should be an easy first step for most runners, but when you apply even this small change in pace to your entire run, it can add up to almost a minute off your 5K time and almost two minutes off your 10K time. That's progress!

Once you have adjusted to this slightly quicker pace for a middle portion of your run, begin to expand the middle portion outward from both ends, so that you are adopting the pace earlier in your run and maintaining it longer into your run. Be patient. Depending on how frequently you run and the distance you are running, you shouldn't be surprised to find that weeks or maybe even a couple of months will pass before you can increase your pace throughout the entire run.

Now that you've been able to cut five to ten seconds from each mile you run, it is time to start the pace training over again, inserting an interval into your run that is another five to ten seconds faster than your new running pace. Of course, there's an end to all of this; you'll know that you've pushed your body as far as it can go when you are simply unable to complete your run at a pace that's any quicker than the one to which you've gradually climbed. You have now found your Middle Pace—the pace at which you'll be able to finish a race, but just barely.

However, as with all training, you don't want to make *every* run into a training run. You'll want to separate your pace training runs from regular runs. If you try to turn every run into a race, you'll soon find your finishing times increasing rather than decreasing. This is because you are overtraining—you're wearing yourself out. You'll put up better times during actual races if you limit your pace training to just once a week, or to short intervals inserted into just a couple of runs each week. That's what it means to respect the lesson of The Middle Way.

Finding The Middle Speed

When doing speed work, you need to keep enough fuel in your tank so that you can muster anywhere from about four to eight speed intervals in a training session. If you go all-out on your first speed interval, you won't have the stamina to do more than another one or two intervals. On the other hand, if your speed interval is not much faster than your ordinary pace, you will not be reaping the benefits that speed work can add to your endurance and speed. How do you know when you've found The Middle Speed?

If you choose to add intervals into your regular runs rather than to set aside a day on a track when you work on nothing but speed, you'll first need to settle on a speed interval distance. Measuring distances is not always easy, and you'll want to do your best to mark out intervals of the same length so that you can find the speed that is right for you.

Here's a technique that has worked for me. First, choose a route into which you'll add speed intervals. Since you will rely on landmarks to measure these intervals, choose a very familiar route, one that's as flat as possible so you don't have the worry that some of the intervals are going uphill while others are going downhill.

Once you've chosen your route, begin to run at your ordinary pace. After five minutes, stop, and look where you are. You're at that bend in the road, or by the big oak tree, or standing on that crack in the pavement. Now start again, still at your ordinary pace, and run for exactly one minute. Stop. Where are you? By that grey rock that looks like Richard Nixon's profile? By the tree with the squirrel's nest on top? At the corner of Main and Elm? You've just marked off your first interval. It took you one minute to run at your ordinary pace, and you'll be cutting that time considerably when you do it at your speed pace. Continue on your run for another five minutes, stop, note where you are, and then run for another minute. Stop. Here's where you end your second interval. Continue in this way until you've partitioned your entire run into five-minute sections separated by one-minute sections. You now know that the intervals you'll speed through on your first training run are all the same length.

With your intervals marked off, you can now find The Middle Speed—the speed that is not too fast for you to maintain during each interval, but just fast enough so that you couldn't possibly do one more. Start by trying to take ten seconds off the minute that it ordinarily takes you to run the first interval. You should be able to do this. Even if it comes very easily to you, do *not* try to do the next interval faster. The point is to run all the intervals at the same accelerated pace. If, by the run's end, you find that you did the intervals without trouble, next time you speed-train, cut the intervals by another five or ten seconds. On the other hand, if you *can't* maintain fifty-second intervals for each of the intervals you have marked, take the intervals a bit slower on your next speed workout.

Whenever I explain how to find your Middle Speed, I'm reminded of that joke about Maxwell House coffee: it's good 'til the last drop, but that last drop is just awful. You'll know you've found your Middle Speed when you can hold that speed until the final foot of that last interval, but that final foot is going to be just awful.

Locating Middle Way Hills

When applied to hill training, The Middle Way can refer either to the length or steepness of the hill. Recently I trained with some friends for a marathon, and to break the monotony of running on the same roads every weekend, we would hop in a car and drive to various state parks. These trips provided us with a nice variety of hills on which to train. Most of these parks offered the challenge of either long or steep hills. Many of the hills could not have been more perfect illustrations of The Middle Way. By the time we reached the crest of a long or steep hill, we were sucking air but not so fatigued that the next hill on the horizon was beyond our ability to climb. These are The Middle Hills you should be looking for. They should be just tough enough to ascend that you feel you can't take another step higher once you've reached the peak.

One park in particular, Devil's Lake, proved to be our undoing. I suppose the park's name should have given us pause. Devil's Lake is nestled between looming cliff faces, and the hills in the area are so long and steep that you'd think some evil force was responsible for their design. We huffed to the top of one hill, nearly rolled down the other side, and jogged slowly up half of the next before giving in and walking the rest of the way, too tired even to hold our heads up. Obviously, these were not The Middle Hills that we were seeking.

When I spent half a year in Sydney, Australia, as a visiting fellow at Sydney University, I lived in a neighborhood that sat on a ridge, with steep hills dropping off each side into the harbor. My first running experiences were not pretty. It seemed that in the course of the forty hours it took me to travel to Sydney I had lost all of my conditioning. Some of my trouble was a matter of acclimating to the climate. The temperature when I stepped off the plane in Sydney was about one hundred degrees warmer than the temperature I had left behind. No kidding. This took some getting used to. But the big difference, of course, was the magnitude of the hills I unexpectedly confronted. These hills were nearly as demonic as the ones that had defeated me at Devil's Lake. Given a choice, they would not be hills on which I would ordinarily attempt to train. In retrospect, I'm glad I didn't have a choice. Acquiring the stamina to run at my usual comfort level took almost two months, but when I returned home I ran my old routes feeling like Superman.

As these examples suggest, The Middle Hills are those that are just long enough or just steep enough to leave you winded, but not defeated. One good indication that you've found your Middle Hill is whether, once you've reached the crest, you're able to continue running down its other side while recovering your breath. If you can do this you're okay. But if you have to stop and rest before taking another step, the hill was too much for you. Look for a shorter hill or a more gradual slope. If you're able to resume your ordinary pace right away, you haven't sufficiently challenged yourself. Go find a bigger hill.

Applying The Middle Way to Low-Distance Training

Low-distance training is not for everyone. In fact, it is probably not for most runners. It's a training program with high demands, promises of high payoffs, and also significant risks of injury. But for people who don't have much time to devote to training, low-distance programs might be the best choice. If you do decide to pursue a low-distance regimen, it is more important than ever to heed The Middle Way. Also important is that you practice the techniques of mindfulness that I discussed in earlier chapters. You need to be completely aware of how your body is responding to the rigors of low-distance workouts. As you train, cast aside all those sensations, feelings, and thoughts that are not directly related to your muscles and tendons and breathing. Doing this creates a kind of early-warning response system. If something goes wrong in your body, you'll know immediately. You'll be able to prevent the injury from becoming something more serious, just as an experienced pilot can pull the plane out of a dive a split second before it's too late.

Low-distance training combines pace training, speed training, and hill training—just not long-distance training. Because a week of low-distance training is much harder on the body than a week of the other sorts of training, you should be prepared to adjust your

Middle Pace, Middle Speed, and Middle Hills accordingly. If you've already gone through the steps I've described to find your Middle Pace, Speed, or Hills, you should begin a low-distance workout by slowing your pace and speed by about 25 percent. For instance, if your Middle Pace is thirty seconds per mile faster than your ordinary pace, your *low-distance* Middle Pace should be about twenty-two seconds faster. If you have been doing an interval in forty-five seconds, increase your time to about forty-nine seconds. This will be your *low-distance* Middle Speed. Likewise, if you have been hill training, look for hills that are not quite as long or as steep as the hills you've been climbing.

FROM THE MOUTHS *of Runners*

BRYNN 24, KENTUCKY "I have trained for so long now, that it is part of my everyday life just like breakfast is. I used to train for racing on the track, but that sort of training and racing left me in a walking boot at least once a year. So now I just train for the sake of training; it keeps me well-balanced."

Some people who low-distance train like to dedicate each run of the week either to pacing, speed, or hills, never combining training methods. If you're accustomed to, say, speed work, you'll find that the first time you try speed work at your low-distance Middle Speed, the intervals will seem easy. Don't succumb to the temptation to increase your speed. Because you are not allowing your body as much rest between training sessions when you low-distance train, you'll soon find that cutting your speed by 25 percent still makes for a hard workout. In fact, after a week or two of low-distance training, you might decide that you need to cut your speed even further. This is fine. If you're mindful of what's happening to your body, and it's telling you that you need to slow down, do it. Ignoring your body's complaints is never a good idea, and especially not when low-distance training.

Others who low-distance train might combine two or even three training methods into a single workout. The nice feature of this approach is that it breaks the monotony that sustained focus on pacing or speed or hills might cause. To try out this method, start your run as you normally would—at your normal pace. When you come to the marker for your first interval, run it at your low-distance Middle Speed: 75 percent of the speed you would use if you were just speed training. Then, instead of dropping back to your normal pace, drop instead to your low-distance Middle Pace and maintain this until you hit the next interval, when you'll increase your speed again to low-distance Middle Speed. At the end of this second interval, reduce your speed to normal pace. You'll now have five minutes to recover until your next interval comes along, at which point you'll start the sequence over again. This is tough going, but you'll never become bored.

Low-distance training requires that you make almost every run into a training run. Typically, you might have four such runs in a week, and then a fifth run at your usual pace. Even this will seem difficult because your body will be tired from your efforts over the previous week. Don't panic! You are not falling out of shape. Over time you'll find that you are in fact moving faster than you used to during your usual runs. "Usual" after several weeks of low-distance training will be faster than what was usual before.

I mentioned earlier that I don't favor low-distance training. That said, I understand why some people may have no choice. If you want to race, you need to train; and if you want to train but have no time, you need to make the most of the time you have.

I suppose that if I were unable to accommodate other forms of training into my schedule, I would also low-distance train. But, given the life I have, low-distance training is simply not The Middle Way for me. It's too extreme. That's why I'd sooner follow the other training methods described here.

Applying The Middle Way to Long-Distance Training

With long-distance training the risk of injury is less than it is with the other forms of training because you're not exposing your body to the sudden stresses of speed or hills. And, if you like running, long distances provide you with more of what you like. Of course, you must draw a line somewhere. You might like chocolate cake too, but this doesn't mean the more the better. Eventually you'll find your chocolate cake limit, and with luck others won't be around to see the results. Likewise, you need to take The Middle Way to heart when searching for the long-distance training regimen that's best for you.

Remember that the goal of long-distance training is not always to race for long distances. If you can run fifteen or twenty miles at your normal pace without a struggle, you'll easily be able to knock minutes off your normal 10K time if it is a 10K race you wish to enter. If it is a marathon you are training for, you shouldn't try to run more than marathon lengths when you long-distance train. I find that a few runs up to twenty-two or twenty-four miles in length are adequate preparation for a marathon, and I sandwich two weeks of runs between these very long runs during which I never run farther than twelve miles. Focus your efforts on building your miles per week rather than miles per run. So, if in a given week I have a twenty-mile run, I don't run more than twenty or so miles throughout the rest of the week. On those weeks when your long run is no more than twelve miles, your other runs combined should not add up to more than thirty miles.

RUNNING **Tip**

If you drive or bike your routes the day before running them in order to confirm their distances, bring along some water bottles to stash along the way, hiding them behind trees, in tall grass, under rocks, and so on. You can then chuck the empties into trash bins along your route, or return later to retrieve them.

Standard wisdom is that long-distance training requires you to run somewhere between forty and fifty miles per week. This might be good advice in general, but The Middle Way for some runners is not The Middle Way for others. When I first began training for marathons, I thought I had to put in forty- to fifty-mile weeks each week if I was going to be successful, which at the time I defined as crossing the finish line while still running, and surviving for at least ten minutes afterward. In subsequent marathons, I've discovered that a weekly maximum of somewhere between thirty-five and forty miles is fine for my goals. In fact, my marathon times became better as I reduced the amount of long-distance training I did. This shows that I was overtraining initially.

Rather than running in accord with The Middle Way, I was working too hard.

So how do you find The Middle Way distance to run each week? The following strategy has worked well for me. I start gradually adding distance to each of my runs, adding the most distance to my Sunday long run. Once I've extended my long runs to about fourteen miles, I'll put two weeks' time between them. In the intervening weeks, I'll make each run about the same length—maybe four runs of seven or eight miles each. When the next big Sunday comes along, I'll add two more miles, running a total of sixteen. Try this, and if you find that these sixteen miles are harder for you to do than the fourteen you did two weeks ago, you're overtraining. Back off on the distances you do in the next two-week period and then try for sixteen again. If you've found your Middle Way, the long run that you do every other week should never seem harder even while it grows in distance. When you've worked your way up to a twenty-mile run, it should be no harder for you than that fourteen-mile run you did a couple of months ago. If it is harder, you've either trained too much or too little. You've stumbled off The Middle Way.

Although long-distance training is a gentler training method, it does demand some precautions that other methods do not. Here are the things to think about before you start a run of more than ten miles:

- You'll need a source of hydration along the way. You should plan a run that has water stops—water fountains, convenience stores, public restroom facilities—or you should bring along your own water or sports drink. Six ounces of fluid every mile or two after the first six, depending on the temperature, should keep you well-hydrated.

- Be sure to apply petroleum jelly to areas of your body that are likely to chafe. Some runners cover their toes and heels with petroleum jelly in order to prevent blisters. Petroleum jelly is a must where the elastic bands of your shorts' lining makes contact in the groin area. Men should consider applying petroleum jelly to their nipples if their shirts tend to become heavy with perspiration. Excessive chafing can cause bleeding, so it's best to prevent!

- Take along some food. Many long-distance runners carry high-protein bars with them in a fanny pack. High-protein energy gels are also popular. I pack a peanut butter and honey sandwich, or sometimes a peanut butter and raisin sandwich. Beats me what the protein, fat, and carbohydrate contents of these sandwiches are, but they seem to work for me.

- Apply sunblock to any exposed areas of skin, and wear a hat and sunglasses. In the past few years, two of my very good running buddies have been treated for melanoma, which is the most lethal kind of skin cancer. These are otherwise very healthy middle-aged men who have spent most of their running years in Wisconsin—far from the equator. Skin cancer is a real threat wherever you run, unless you run before the sun rises or after it sets. Take care!

Learning about Yourself Through Training

Is there any reason to train if you are not interested in racing? You might think that the answer to this question is an obvious and thunderous NO! Training isn't for everyone, and there are plenty of reasons to run even if you never plan to race, but most runners who have spent time training believe they have learned something from the experience.

FROM THE MOUTHS *of Runners*

DIANNE 52, CONNECTICUT "I'm not much into training or racing. For me, running is an end in itself—a time to put aside the worries of routine life and commune with nature."

I think there are good reasons to train regardless of whether you ever plan to enter a race.

Zen, we have seen, emphasizes the importance of mental discipline. The disciplined mind is preferable to the lazy or disorganized mind. A mind sharpened by Zen can shed negative emotions like anger, frustration, and jealousy. The Zen mind is capable of finding bliss even in the harshest conditions. Mindfulness and right effort, we have seen, are indispensable features of a mind that cannot be disturbed. But the ability to recognize and distinguish all the thoughts and feelings that run through your mind, and then to expel the unwanted ones, is something you can attain only through hard work. Interestingly, however—and this is where training comes in—this hard work is often easier when negative feelings are most prominent—most conspicuous.

As an analogy, suppose you had a pile of apples and wanted to sort the good ones from the bad ones. This job would be much more difficult if the good and bad apples looked similar to each other than it would be if they looked very different. If the good apples were smooth, red, and firm while the bad apples were brown, soft, and full of worm holes, the task of separating them would be very easy.

Negative feelings, when they are not very strong, can consume you before you become aware of their presence. This is one of the reasons that mindfulness is so difficult. Mindfulness requires you to recognize each of the thoughts and feelings that is present in your mind, but if these thoughts and feelings are dim or weak, they can go unrecognized even while doing damage to your psyche. You won't have this problem with the negative emotions you experience while training. Believe me: if you are not used to training, there will be no mistaking the aches, pains, desire to quit, and feelings of uncertainty or inadequacy that accompany your first few trials.

BUDDHA **Says**

No one saves us but ourselves. No one can and no one may. We ourselves must walk the path.

This, you may be surprised to learn, puts you in an enviable position. Chances are your mind will now be more transparent to you than it ever has been in the past. No need for you to hunt the crevasses of your soul searching for thoughts and feelings that may or may not be present. That pain is right *there*—announcing its presence with all the fanfare of an Independence Day fireworks display.

That intense desire to give up is right there in front of you, shouting "Quit! Quit! Quit!"

The more prominent and conspicuous these bad apples are, the easier it is for you to recognize them and deal with them in ways discussed in earlier chapters. Label them. Make them tangible. Give them substance. Then throw them away.

Use right effort to put positive thoughts in their place: "I'm almost to the top of the hill. I can make it. This hill is not as tough as I am." Or "One hundred feet to go. I've never run this fast for this long. I can make it." Or "Fifteen down and only five miles to go. The last five are nothing. I've always been able to run five miles."

The reason to train, even if you are not planning to race, is to experience this rare moment of mental transparency—of having your mind open before you like a large-print book. You'll learn a lot about yourself and how to go about disciplining your mind under these circumstances.

Perhaps more important, your practice with these conspicuous negative emotions will help you become better at recognizing those that are less obvious, that speak in only whispers. The more familiar you become with good and bad apples, the better you'll become at sorting them, even when the differences in appearance between the apples become less obvious. This is the usual way that learning a skill progresses. You start with the easy cases, and when you are competent in dealing with these, you're able to move on to harder cases that at one time were beyond your ability. Once you become proficient at dealing with the obvious negative emotions and thoughts that arise during training, you'll find yourself able to manage others that you might not have been able to identify before.

CHAPTER 6
THE ZEN OF RACING

You've trained. Now it is time to apply all that hard work. In this chapter you'll see how a Zen perspective can ease the anxiety racers often face in the days leading up to the big event and in the moments before the starting gun sounds. You'll also learn how Zen can help you during the race itself, and what Zen can do for you after the race has ended and you suddenly find yourself aimless, with no immediate running goal in sight. I hope the advice in this chapter makes racing as pleasurable for you as it has been for me.

Handling a Body at Rest but a Mind in Turmoil

If you've found your Middle Way in training, your body should be tired, but not completely spent. Your muscles should ache, but just dully and not to the point of distraction. If walking down a staircase makes you wince, you've trained too hard. You've demanded too much from your muscles. If you can bend over to pick up the newspaper from the front walk without registering any discomfort at all, you haven't been training hard enough. Your body should be telling you that it is aware of the extra load you've made it carry these past few months, but by now it is used to it and doesn't mind so much. When I first started to teach and a seventy-five-minute class period opened up before me like a bottomless abyss, two hundred eyes all aimed at me, pens in hand poised to write down whatever came out of my mouth, I was terrified. Now, after years of experience, I manage. I'm still not completely at ease, but I can handle the situation. That's how your body should feel about the training it has undertaken. It was very tough at first, and it's still tough, but now it can be managed.

Ideally, you've reached this point about two weeks before a race of fifteen miles or more, and about seven to ten days before a shorter race. You'll need this period between the end of your training and the start of the race to taper—to reduce your workouts so that your body is fresh and strong on race day. Aaah, you might be thinking. A week or two just to relax and recuperate. A few easy runs to keep the body loose. Nothing too strenuous. What a treat! Right? Wrong. For most runners, those one or two weeks between the end of training and the start of the race are anything but relaxing. In fact, these weeks might seem harder to get through than the entire duration of your training period. Here's where your other kind of training, your Zen training, can be of service.

Following the Rigors of Tapering

Let's first figure out why the tapering period is so hard for many runners to bear.

There are several factors at work that, when combined, can make taper time seem more like torture time:

1. A restless body that has become used to strenuous exertions and is now unwilling to take it easy;
2. Nervous excitement that race day is nearly upon you—the culmination of months of training; and
3. Worries that you will not be able to accomplish the racing goals you have set yourself.

From a Zen perspective, these three obstacles are mental afflictions, and like all such afflictions, they can be tamed with the proper sort of mental focus. Fully understanding these afflictions is a first step toward dealing with them in a Zen way.

Dealing with Restless Bodies, Restless Minds

You are now in superb condition. You are fitter than you have been for months, or maybe years, or maybe ever. Your body has adjusted to the routines of a strenuous training regimen. You feel like a superhero, able to outrun bullets, stop locomotives, and jump over tall buildings in a single bound. How can you be expected at this point just to call it quits, like a racehorse sent to pasture? Those running shoes belong on your feet, not in the closet. That specially designed wicking fabric belongs on your back, not in a drawer or draped over a chair. Your fingers itch to hit the *chrono* button on your watch. You pace nervously back and forth on your front step like a caged tiger at feeding time. When your spouse proposes a drive to the grocery store to pick up a gallon of milk, you eagerly offer to run (literally) over to the store yourself. And then run home carrying a gallon of milk? Sure—why not?

Simply put, your efforts over the past few months have created a monster of sorts. Your body is no longer just a body; it is a well-oiled running machine, and it is not going to rest without a fight. It is not designed to rest. You made it this way, and now you face the consequences. Your job now is to keep your wits about you while your body is chomping at the bit to *move, move, move*.

Surviving the Nervous Wait

As any new parent will tell you, one of the worst parts of a pregnancy involves those last few days, when the baby could appear at any time. At that point, a pregnant couple knows that the event they've been preparing for these past nine months is finally at hand, and now the anticipation is driving them crazy. Racers experience the same kind of before-the-event anxiety, although perhaps not to such an extreme extent.

BUDDHA **Says**

It is a person's own mind, not his enemy or foe, that lures him to evil ways.

The worst pre-race anxiety I have ever felt occurred during the days before an Ironman race. I had never raced an Ironman before—in fact, I had never raced *any* triathlon before. I hoped, however, that the year I had just spent training would be enough to carry me through the 2.4 miles of swimming, 112 miles of cycling, and 26.2 miles of running that is an Ironman. I wanted more than anything else just to have the thing over and done with. Was I stressed out? You bet I was. I tossed and turned at night, unable to stanch the nervous energy and excitement that was keeping me awake.

When sleep did come, my dreams were always of race day catastrophes: I got to the starting line and realized I had forgotten my wetsuit and bathing suit and so had to swim naked; someone had strapped a wagon to the back of my bicycle that I didn't have time to remove, so I had to tow it the whole way while spectators tossed watermelons into it; when I was finally done biking, I got to change into my marathon clothes only to discover that someone had tied knots in the laces of my running shoes that I couldn't loosen. To this day, my stomach still tightens when I think back to what I was feeling during those two weeks of "rest and relaxation" before the race.

Obviously, your performance on race day is going to suffer if you can't control your anxieties during the tapering period leading up to the race. Learning to manage your mind, to keep your anxieties from running unchecked like a savage pack of wolves among a herd of deer, is something you must master.

Handling Self-Doubt

The anxieties I just discussed are rooted in *excitement*. You've prepared for the race, done everything within your power to ensure a successful completion, and now you just want it to be over. Like that pregnant couple in their ninth month, you just can't wait another minute for the big day, and the anticipation is killing you.

But there is another kind of anxiety, less healthy than the sort that derives from excitement. This is the anxiety of self-doubt.

Self-doubt is not limited to first-time racers. All of the runners I know—*all* of them—have, before one race or another, expressed concerns that they didn't train long enough, or that they over-trained, or that they didn't do enough training in hot conditions like those predicted for race day, or that they missed a training run four weeks ago and so they can't possibly be prepared. And, of these self-doubters I've known, how many actually finished the races they started? *All* of them.

But this does not mean that the feelings of uncertainty these runners experienced during their tapering periods were without cost. Chances are, they would have raced better if they hadn't lacked confidence in themselves in the days prior to the race. They would have rested better, slept better, eaten better, and felt, in general, happier. Going into the race with a positive attitude would, probably, have changed the way they ran the race.

BUDDHA **Says**

> There is nothing more terrible than the habit of doubt. Doubt separates people. It is a poison that ruins friendships and breaks up pleasant relations. It is a thorn that irritates and hurts. It is a sword that kills.

If you begin a race believing that you may not finish it, you might run tentatively, perhaps adopting a pace slower than one you are capable of, or you might have to fight a constant struggle against your uncertainties in order to keep the pace you've trained so hard to maintain.

It's only natural that you should have some performance worries as race day approaches. You've worked hard—very hard—and you have set difficult goals for yourself. There are a lot of "what ifs" to consider, a lot of things that can go wrong. This is true of anything in life worth striving for. But these misgivings become hazardous when they overwhelm you and weaken your determination to achieve your objectives.

Making Zen Part of Your Tapering Period

Now that we have a clearer picture of the mental afflictions that can prevent runners from relaxing and enjoying the week or two before a race, we can begin to approach these problems from a Zen point of view. Restlessness, nervous excitement, and self-doubt are symptoms of a mind in disorder, of a mind that needs to be reined in and subdued. For this, there is no better tool than Zen meditation. Despite the difficulty that meditation often presents the untrained mind, it is a great addition to your tapering period and one that I urge you to adopt. Remember that the goal of meditation is to empty your mind. And, although this emptiness lasts for only as long as you meditate, afterward you will feel rested. Your mind will have had a reprieve from the anxieties that have been boiling within it. Also, having emptied your mind, you should be able to take a new perspective on the anxieties that have been plaguing you. You'll have an easier time recognizing them, distinguishing them, labeling them, and, finally, casting them aside.

A perfect moment to practice meditation is during the time that you would ordinarily be exercising. This is time that you have already set aside for yourself. You are used to being on your own during this time, free from family and work obligations, and you are used to doing something constructive with this time. A lot of the restlessness you feel as a result of having reduced your exercise schedule exists because you have not replaced your exercise with anything else. Let meditation—a kind of mental exercise—take the place of the physical exercise that you normally do during this time of day.

When you tell yourself that you will now meditate during a period when ordinarily you would run, you also *regiment* your meditation sessions. The idea of regimentation is familiar to any runner. Having a running schedule—a routine that varies little from week to week—is actually very important for runners. A runner's body acclimates itself to the days, times, and durations that a running schedule enforces, and is thus naturally prepared to run when called to do so. But regimentation is also useful as a means to motivate yourself.

FROM THE MOUTHS *of Runners*

ALISON 22, MINNESOTA "For me, it helps to be signed up for a race because then it makes me want to get out and go running so I know that when it comes time to race, I did all I could to train and run my best."

If you haven't settled on a particular time that is especially dedicated to running, telling yourself that *now* is the time to run becomes much harder. "Why now?" those devilish voices inside your head might ask. Why not after I finish reading the paper, watching this TV show, doing this crossword? On the other hand, if a schedule tells you to run tomorrow morning at seven, you do it. Why? Because the schedule tells you to do it, and you will not have become involved in some other activity that you can't put to the side.

So, once you replace running with meditating, you'll be able to approach meditation with the same rigid discipline that helps you to run. Of course, you don't need to completely fill a running slot with meditation—an hour of meditation is *much* harder than an hour of running. Instead, plan to spend about fifteen minutes meditating. Find a quiet room where you will be free from distractions. Choose a chair where you can sit comfortably, but not too comfortably. Remember, you want to avoid those sleeping hazards that I've mentioned before. The point of meditation is not to sleep! In fact, the point is not even to relax. The goal of meditation is to calm your mind, but you can attain this goal only through prolonged concentration.

Easing Pre-Race Jitters with Meditation

Close your eyes and begin to silently count your breaths. Inhale (one), exhale (two), and so on until you reach ten and then begin again. As you do this, the negative emotions that have been making you tense will try their best to push their way into the front of your mind. Your body will be telling you that it needs to go for a run.

ZEN **Practice**

Try to list all the concerns, worries, and anxieties that are making you uncomfortable or sleepless during your taper period. Once you have this list, examine each of the items it contains. On what unhealthy attachments do these items rest? Try using mindfulness and right effort to soften their sting.

A thought about the impending race will flit into your consciousness and bring with it a burst of disruptive anticipation, as well, perhaps, as feelings of self-doubt or dread. At first, you'll have a hard time suppressing these worries. They will overwhelm the beam of concentration that you have focused on your breathing. You'll lose your count. There is a struggle going on for nothing less than the control of your mind.

FROM THE MOUTHS *of Runners*

STEVE 49, NEW YORK "I just completed my first marathon, but it was almost a little anticlimactic. I had the training miles in, and after twenty-one or twenty-two miles it was clear that I would have no problem finishing. The training was the 'event.' The marathon turned out to be little more than validation of sufficient training. (But I was still happy.)"

Once you recognize that your mind is giving ground to unwelcome thoughts, get back on count. It helps to remember that odd numbers label inhalations and even numbers are for exhalations. Crucially, you should not try to fight against the worries that come uninvited into your consciousness. This will only produce frustration. Instead, as you continue to count your breaths, briefly, and without much thought, notice your worries. Think of them as birds that fly past far in the distance. You notice them, but just casually, without much interest. Your main focus should, as always, be on your breathing. As you concentrate on the air moving in and out of your lungs, the worries that you allow to fly across your mental screen will become less *engaging*. Their sharp edges will erode and smooth. They will no longer "catch" your mind as they glide past.

The more you practice meditation, the easier it becomes. If on your first try you are unable to vanquish the thoughts that trouble you, or can do so for only a minute or less, don't become discouraged. Try again in an hour, or wait until tomorrow.

You'll find that as you gain proficiency in meditation, the anxieties that are preventing you from relaxing during your recovery period will gradually ease. Feelings of anxiety are often like ferocious dogs. If you show weakness, they will tear into you. But if you show them that you are in charge, they will leave you alone. As you meditate, you confront your anxieties fearlessly, and this makes them easier to stare down even after you have finished meditating.

Waiting for the Starting Gun

You've made it through the tapering period. Ideally, meditation over the past week or so has provided some relief from the restlessness, nervous excitement, and sporadic self-doubt that many runners experience while they await the start of the race. In any event, whatever stresses you suffered during the long wait don't matter now. That's behind you. You're now yards from the starting line. You have safety-pinned your number bib to your shirt, looped a timing chip over your shoelaces, greeted friends and acquaintances you've made on the road, and are now just trying to remain calm for the next ten or fifteen minutes until the crack of the starting gun pierces the air.

These final minutes are often excruciating. If the tapering period is like the last days of a pregnancy, the minutes before the start of the race are like those last few pushes before the baby squirms red-faced into the world. You know it's coming. What's taking so long? Let's get going! My knees weaken just thinking about these sorts of moments. But now is not the time to give in to the pressure. Do NOT sprint up and down the block trying to burn off nervous energy. You'll need all the energy you can muster when you're actually racing. Do NOT decide that you haven't stretched enough and you need to stretch some more. This is not the time to tear a muscle. Do NOT run in circles, waving your hands in the air and shouting obscenities at the clouds. You'll look like an idiot.

DO find a place apart from other runners and away from milling crowds of supporters. A doorway usually works well if you're in an urban area. A shady spot beneath a tree is also a good target. Once you've separated yourself from others, you'll have an easier time calming yourself down. Don't waste your time trying to meditate. Unless you're a Buddhist monk, long-practiced in meditation, you'll find the present environment just too stimulating for meditation. So, instead of meditating, begin to breathe deeply as you would when you meditate, but don't bother to count your breaths. Instead, think about something that will distract you from the exertions that the race will soon require. Recall with as much graphic detail as possible the very first training session you did in preparation for this race. How far did you run? At what pace? Was it raining? The more details you can remember, the better you'll be able to recover the feelings you had while you ran, or sprinted, or climbed hills. These feelings are what you're after right now. How did your legs feel as you quickened your pace through an interval or chugged up a steep incline? Was your heart beating hard at the end of the interval? Were your breaths coming in gasps?

Now bring to mind your very last training session. Think about the progress you made between the first and final sessions. Those hills that almost killed you are no longer steep enough to wear you out. You now have to climb them several times to feel the same exhaustion that a single climb used to cause. The speed intervals you started with are now too short or too slow to make your heart pound. Those pacing runs that left you panting a few months ago were slower than the pace you now run ordinarily—for leisure!

The point of this exercise is twofold. First, you want to keep your mind from becoming absorbed in the frenetic goings-on all around you. The other racers are just as nervous as you are—more so probably given the mental discipline you have been working to acquire. Nervousness like this is viral—it can spread. If you are surrounded by people who are hopping about, doing jumping jacks, skipping up and down staircases, and so on, there is a good chance you will become infected with the same kind of anxiety that's driving their behavior. This is why you need to isolate yourself from the starting-line masses.

FROM THE MOUTHS *of Runners*

DONNA 36, AUSTRALIA "I recently did my fastest time at the 'Balmoral Burn,' an uphill sprint for charity. I was so nervous beforehand that my butterflies carried me up the hill!!"

But second, and more important, concentrating on your first and last training sessions will promote feelings of confidence, assurance, and pride. These feelings are all justified! Think about what you have accomplished over the past many weeks. You have turned a novice runner into an experienced one, or an experienced runner into a sleek machine. Speeds and distances that were once outside your reach are now in your domain. You have met your goals. You have, in a very real sense, already won this race. All that's left to do is run it. That's the attitude that you should take with you once the starting gun sounds.

Racing in the Moment

Let's just say it and be done with it. Racing hurts. But here's another truth: having put in the effort to prepare for a race and then not giving it your all hurts even more. The first kind of hurt goes away in hours or a day. The second kind of hurt can last a lifetime. I have a friend who spent months training for a marathon. We trained together some of the time, and I witnessed firsthand how hard he was working and how well he was progressing. By the time he began to taper in preparation for the race, he was definitely ready. He was feeling confident. All systems were go. But something happened during the last six miles of the marathon. For some reason, he lost his mojo. Instead of keeping his eyes on the prize, he started to think about the aches and cramps that had been accumulating over the past few miles. He began to think about how nice it would be just to slow down, take it easy, maybe walk for a spell. He ended up walking and jogging the final four miles.

There is no shame in walking part of a race if this is what you must do to finish it. On any given race day, no matter how well prepared you are, you might find yourself unable to run the entire distance. Things like that just happen. Better to walk than to run if you're really hurting. But this is not the situation my friend found himself in. He could have run the entire marathon, but his drive to do so collapsed somewhere along the way. He gave into the pain when he could have kept going. Now he can't forgive himself.

My friend's performance in that race haunts him, even though he's since run other marathons and has exceeded the goals he set for himself. I don't want to exaggerate the distress my friend feels. His failure to live up to his expectations during a single race hasn't destroyed his life. Still, he sees himself as having failed in that race, and, he'll now freely admit, the weight of that failure is much worse than the pain he experienced as he ran.

RUNNING **Tip**

If you need hydration during the race, walking through the water stop is better than running through it. If you try to drink while you're running, there's a good chance that you'll choke on the water and lose more time than if you had simply walked through the station. Also, if you haven't trained with a sports drink, stick to water during the race. A race is not a good time to find out how your body reacts to a sports drink.

If you don't want to end up like my friend, you need to build the mental discipline that will keep you racing even as those little voices in your head tell you how nice it would be just to slow down a bit, enjoy the scenery, smell the flowers, and so on. These little voices, which speak in a seductive purr and do their best to entice you from the goal you have worked so hard to complete, are what you must learn to master. But the best way to master these voices is not to ignore them or try to silence them. Rather, you must see to it that they have nothing to complain about. You'll do this by *racing in the moment*.

Entering the Zone

The first few minutes of the race are all hustle and bustle. You'll be seeking paths around slower runners who started in front of you, and faster runners will be jostling to pass you from behind. Depending on the distance of the race and the size of the field, several minutes may go by before you are finally able to adopt the pace that you hope to keep for most of the race.

Once you drop into your pace, it's time to *enter the zone*. It's time to empty your mind and let your body do the task that you've trained it to do.

Pick a spot on the ground ten or fifteen feet in front of you. Or, if you are in a crowded field of runners, you might focus on that bright red hat or those fluorescent green running shorts up ahead. If you do focus on other runners, try to find runners who are ahead of you but keeping roughly the same pace as you. Now begin to count your steps as I described in Chapter 4. Every time your left foot hits the ground, count. When you reach ten, start over again.

BUDDHA **Says**

There are only two mistakes one can make along the road to truth: not going all the way and not starting.

Concentrate on the feeling of your feet hitting the ground. You should try to experience each impact of foot on ground as a unique event, and, in fact, each one is. Zen Buddhists emphasize the uniqueness of experience. What's past is no longer, and what's to be is not yet. There is only now. Never before has your foot hit this ground at this time, and never again will it. Make yourself aware of every individual impact. Feel your foot expand into your shoe as the force of its contact with the ground flattens your sole. Is there a pebble on the ground that you feel through your shoe? Is your foot level when it hits, or is it on an incline?

As you reduce your attention into a narrow beam and aim it just on the sensations you experience with each step, you'll find those little voices have nothing to say to you. There is nothing for them to talk about. They can't complain about cramping, or blisters, or burning lungs, because you are not aware of these. All you are aware of is your feet hitting the ground, and who wants to talk about that?

You will know you have entered the zone when you are able to block from your thoughts everything but the sensations of your feet hitting the ground. This state of unawareness is like the state you strive for when meditating. And, if you've been successful in your meditation practices, you'll have an easier time finding it as you race. However, even if you find yourself unable to enter the zone completely, or if you can enter the zone only for a minute or two at a time, you'll find some benefit merely in trying. The mental effort that you spend as you try to find the zone can provide a needed distraction from the strain that your body is presently undergoing. Just as the sound of jackhammers from the construction site next door "go away" when you become completely absorbed in a book or a movie, so too will your pains fade as you concentrate on entering the zone.

Embracing the Pain

Instead of emptying your mind of the negative thoughts that creep into your consciousness as you run your race, it may be easier for you to *embrace* them. If you make yourself fully aware of discomforts as you experience them, you can turn them into something else. You can make them distinct from yourself, and thus something that you can handle, pack up, and throw away. Then those nasty little voices that try to convince you to slow down, have a spot of tea, and walk the rest of the way will have to find something else to talk about.

To embrace your pain, you will use the mindfulness techniques that are at the heart of Zen. The "nice" thing about pain is that it is very conspicuous. While uncovering the resentment you've held toward your mother might take years of self-inspection or the assistance of a therapist, there's nothing subtle about pain. Pain does not camouflage itself like a green caterpillar on a blade of grass. It does not try to disguise itself as something harmless or pleasant. It is what it is and there's no mistaking it.

ZEN **Practice**

Next time you find yourself hurting as you run, focus on the hurt, making it the sole item in your mind. Concentrate on it intensely, as if you were inspecting it with a magnifying glass. You'll find that when you do this, you can separate yourself from the pain, so that it doesn't bother you as much.

I like to talk about pain when I teach my Introduction to Philosophy class. The philosopher Descartes noticed that we can have knowledge of things like pain in a way that we can't have knowledge of things in the world outside us. Suppose I believe that there is a tree in front of me, or that I am sitting on a chair, or that the sun is setting. There's a chance, however small, that all of these beliefs are actually false. Perhaps I have been hypnotized or drugged, or I am dreaming. Then, the tree that I think I see in front of me, the chair I think I am sitting on, the sun I think is setting, might not really be present, or might not be as I believe them to be.

On the other hand, I can't be wrong that I'm feeling pain when I seem to be feeling pain. There's no difference between seeming to feel pain and actually feeling pain. Seeming to feel pain hurts just as much as actually feeling pain! If Descartes is right, this could explain why it is easier to be fully aware of the pain you are feeling than it is to be fully aware of other emotions.

As you struggle to maintain your pace and to run those extra miles, there will come a time when your body's complaints are hard to ignore. Perhaps you've been in the zone for a while, but you are now having difficulty staying focused on your strides. Those voices, silent until now, start to demand your attention. "Hey," they yell, "You! Aren't you getting tired of all this? Wouldn't you like to take a break? I know you're hurting. We can feel it. Slow down!"

When the voices start to clamor like this, there's little hope of completely blocking them from your mind. Instead, you need to open your arms wide and give them a big hug. Okay—not literally, of course. But you should now turn the full fury of the Zen focus that you've been developing directly onto those irritations, qualms, and aches that are singing in your ears. You have a cramp in your side? Be that cramp. Concentrate on it. Where exactly is it? Is it sharp? Does it stab? Where is its point? Visualize it. Of course, this will *not* make the cramp go away. Zen is not magic. However, diverting all your attention to the cramp itself, rather than allowing your mind to drift to questions like "When will it go away?" "How much longer will it hurt?" and so on should make the pain bearable. You must try to see the cramp for what it really is. It is nothing more than an ache in your side. It is *not* a reason to slow down or give up. If you do slow down, this is how *you have chosen* to respond to the cramp. You have turned the cramp into something that it is not: a reason to quit.

Once you've taken care of that cramp, you can start to work on the other irritants that those voices are telling you about. You have a blister on the tip of your toe? Which toe? Try to come up with ten words that describe the sensation you are feeling most precisely. Sharp? Dull? Throbbing? Don't use words like *excruciating* or *unbearable*. Think about what you are saying when you use words like those. To describe the blister's pain as excruciating or unbearable is to describe how you are reacting to the pain. You are no longer describing the pain itself.

FROM THE MOUTHS *of Runners*

GABE 42, MASSACHUSETTS "I have trained for two marathons and both times felt mostly pride in the accomplishment. I enjoy the feeling of picking an attainable goal and then sticking with it—distance, time, and so forth. It's nice to have some part of my life that is challenging but has such clearly defined intermediate goals and end points . . . as opposed to a lot of what happens at work."

Here's an analogy to help illustrate this point. For decades, my wife and I have been engaged in a battle about whether or not Woody Allen movies are funny. I think they are (the early ones, at any rate), but my wife does not. Obviously, Woody Allen movies can't be funny and not funny at the same time. What I am really saying to my wife when I proclaim Woody Allen movies to be funny is that *I* think they're funny. She's telling me that *she* does not think they're funny. Of course, this means that the argument I have with my wife is completely pointless and a waste of time, but what fun is marriage if you can't engage in pointless and time-wasting activities with your spouse?

But that blister is no more excruciating all on its own than a Woody Allen movie is funny all on its own. It's just a blister. If it is excruciating, that's on you. That's something you are adding to the blister, just as I am adding something to Woody Allen movies when I find them funny. Try to see the blister from the perspective of an outsider—see it in the third person rather than the first person. Once you see it this way, you can ask yourself whether the sac of fluid on your toe is in fact more than a sac of fluid, and whether the pain it is causing is more than just a feeling. Are these things more than what they are? Of course not. Are they reasons to quit? No way.

Minding Your Body

A word of caution: the sorts of aches and pains I have been discussing are no more than irritants. Cramps in your side will go away on their own. Blisters heal without leaving behind any lasting damage. As you trained for this race, you became very familiar with all the minor bothers that typically afflict your body—the aches and pains you suffer in any given moment within your body's normal repertoire of experiences. *These* are the bothers to which you should not allow yourself to succumb. However, during the race, if you find yourself with pain in places that have not hurt before, or if old pains are suddenly more acute and intense than they've ever been, *stop immediately and give yourself a minute to rest. Seek medical attention if the pains do not quickly ease.* Once you've rested and the pain has subsided, start again, but slowly. Don't continue if the pain returns.

There are two sides to mindfulness. On the one hand, you can use mindfulness to isolate and disarm the minor pains that afflict runners. On the other hand, mindfulness enhances your awareness of painful sensations. Mindfulness can, quite literally, be a lifesaver in this second instance. When mindfulness exposes previously unknown and potentially dangerous aches and pains, do not ignore them. Take whatever actions are appropriate and do this immediately.

Moving On When the Race Is Over

You've crossed the finish line! Maybe you've met the goal you set yourself. Maybe you've bettered it, or fallen short. The most important thing is that you've done your best.

Ideally, there should be no second-guessing your performance, no "if only I had tried harder" thoughts, no disappointment in the amount of effort you put into the race. Now, finally, you can revel in the joy of seeing that your months of hard work came to fruition. No matter whether you've just run a distance of five miles or twenty-six miles, you can take pride in your accomplishment.

Now what? You go home, shower, maybe take a nap, have a beer, treat yourself to some ice cream (but not while you're drinking beer—yuck). And then? At the risk of stretching the pregnancy analogy too far, some runners feel a kind of *postpartum* depression after a race. They become depressed because all that they've worked for is now behind them. Without a race to motivate them, some runners become mopey and listless. They begin to lose the conditioning that came with all that training. Most runners just don't have an easy time slowing down.

The Buddhist idea of right effort can make a big difference in the lives of runners who experience this kind of post-race depression. Right effort, you will recall, is the practice of replacing negative emotions with positive ones. The first step is to use mindfulness to figure out exactly which negative emotions you experience. The second step is then to replace these negative emotions with positive ones.

Using Mindfulness and Right Effort to Deal with Post-Racing Blues

Let's start with mindfulness. You might recognize that the race's completion has left you out of sorts. But why, exactly? After my first race I remember feeling at a loss for things to do with the extra time that had gone into training. My rigidly scheduled life was now full of gaps and holes. I also remember feeling disgusted with myself as my conditioning began to slide. Physical feats that I could perform without a thought when I was in top form became, not hard exactly, but noticeable. For instance, I noticed that the five flights of stairs I would daily climb to my office became steadily more difficult to surmount. Also, I found that the pleasure I took in running began to wane because I felt that I had no goal to work toward. What was the point?

In retrospect, all this was silly, and I feel like a whiner now when I put these thoughts to paper. But it's easier to see this with hindsight. At the time, I knew only that running had lost some of its spark for me. The solution was obvious. I either had to set my sights on a new race, or I had to realize that there are reasons to run even when there is no race on the immediate horizon.

If I had known more about Zen, I would have practiced right effort on the feelings I experienced. Instead of feeling aimless, I would have shifted my thoughts to feel excitement at the prospect of searching for a new goal. Accomplishing a goal is not an end; it is a beginning. It involves the freedom to set off in search of new goals, perhaps even more challenging goals. This was the path I finally settled on. From 10Ks I went on to marathons and then to the Ironman.

Instead of feeling despair at my loss in conditioning, I would have seen this decline in my fitness as a natural and regenerative response to the previous months' exertions. Even professional racers need time to recuperate between events. More harm than good comes from ceaseless training. With Zen, I would have been glad to have reached such a high level of fitness in the first place. I would have recognized that a temporary decrease in fitness doesn't have to be permanent. Having achieved a high level of fitness once, I knew what I had to do to get it back.

I also realize now that I was wrong to believe that running had to serve some purpose—that without a race in the future there was no point to running. Pleasure is reason enough to engage in some actions. I was mistaken to think that running for the sake of running was no longer enough. It was enough before I started racing, and it would be enough even were I never to race again.

RUNNING **Tip**

Be sure to ice right away whatever is aching after a race. You've pushed yourself hard, and if you don't ice now, you'll ache tomorrow.

Now when I finish a race, I do not have to go through the steps of right effort to feel happy and fulfilled. After a while, the lessons we learn from experimenting with right effort kick in automatically. Right effort creates a *tendency* toward optimism, toward seeing the glass as half-full. A tendency toward optimism becomes especially invaluable for a runner when issues come along that are more serious than post-race blahs. Injury, aging, and other unfortunate events will eventually take their toll on all runners. Learning to deal with these undesirable inevitabilities is essential to a runner's well-being, and we'll take a look at that next.

CHAPTER 7
THE ZEN GUIDE TO INJURY AND AGING

Just a few weeks after my thirty-eighth birthday, I sustained my first serious injury. As any runner knows, a "serious" injury is any injury that prevents you from running. All other injuries are simply not serious. Thus, you may have broken your hand, lacerated your cornea, or blown the nose off your face with firecrackers (don't try this at home), but these injuries are not serious, because none of them prevent you from running. Serious injuries typically involve your feet or legs, and sometimes your hips or back.

My injury took place on a squash court. Squash is a game of quickness and agility, talents not directly related to but somehow developed by long-distance running. As I stretched to return a shot, I felt a pain in my left calf, as if my opponent had whacked me with his racquet. Next thing I knew, I was lying on the floor, trying to figure out who was screaming. The screaming, of course, was coming from my mouth. And that water streaming down my cheeks was coming from my eyes.

The emergency room doctor suspected a torn gastrocnemius muscle, two of which compose the calf muscles on each leg. He didn't need to say this is a very painful sort of injury. He wrote me a prescription for codeine and told me to see my sports medicine physician ASAP.

The next day, my sports med doctor confirmed that I had torn both gastrocnemius muscles in my left leg. The pain of the injury paled, however, to what came next. "This sort of injury," he solemnly intoned, "is very common among middle-aged athletes." Middle-aged? Me? When had that happened? Sure, doubling my age would make me seventy-six, which is roughly a life span, so, technically, he was correct. But me? Middle-aged? I couldn't believe what I was hearing. To find a silver lining in this grim assessment, I grabbed hold of the word *athlete*. The category of middle-aged athlete still beat the label of middle-aged couch potato.

The prognosis for my injury was disheartening. I would spend a minimum of four months on crutches. Then it would be another two months before I could think about running again.

That's six months without running. One hundred-eighty-three days.

I began to think about that rule of thumb that haunts every runner. Every week of running you miss requires two weeks more to regain the fitness you've lost. I would need an entire year to rebuild the fitness I lost after six months without running. Worse, I would probably sink to a base level of fitness even before the end of six months of inactivity. By the time I could run again, I'd be starting all over. My entire life of running up until that moment would be gone without a trace. I'd be like any newbie just starting to run when next I laced up my shoes.

BUDDHA **Says**

The secret of health for mind and body is not to mourn for the past, nor to worry about the future, but to live the present moment wisely and earnestly.

Fortunately, I had Zen to help me deal with my injury and the following periods of recovery and rebuilding. Zen is the ideal companion to the ailing runner—who we will each be on some occasion. Zen is also the perfect companion to the aging runner, who must learn to accept that previous paces and distances are no longer within reach. Let's take a look at how Zen can help you through the inevitabilities of injury and aging that runners so often find hard to accept.

Facing Injuries

While it may be possible to experience a lifetime of running without ever suffering an injury, at one time or another, all of my running acquaintances have had to sit out a week or more as a result of some kind of injury. Some injuries are not serious and go away quickly with ice and rest. Others, like my calf tear, require extended periods of rest and physical therapy, possibly combined with ultrasound treatments. Still worse are injuries that require surgery followed by a lengthy convalescence. This section examines the injuries runners are likely to face at some point in their journey. Most are easily treated and require just one or two weeks of rest. Without proper care and attention, however, some of these injuries can become more serious.

Understanding Common Running Injuries

Runners sustain many sorts of injuries, but some are much more common than others. There's a good chance that you'll experience at least one of the following.

Shin Splints

Shin splints involve the pain many runners experience in the front of the leg between the foot and the knee. The most typical cause of shin splints is tight calf muscles, which force the muscles in the front of your leg to work too hard. While this injury is not terribly serious, it is painful, and you may need to cut back on distances or take a week or two off from running altogether. Stretching the calf muscles before a run can help prevent shin splints, and using the RICE treatment (Rest, Ice, Compression, Elevation) after a run will reduce the pain.

Plantar Fasciitis

This one is easy to spot. If you scream when you step out of bed, chances are high that you have overstretched or torn the fascia (connecting tissue) that stretches from your heel, across the bottom of your arch, to the ball of your foot. As you run, you'll feel a sharp pain in your heel or arch. Like shin splints, RICE will help with the pain, and calf stretches will help prevent future injuries, as will some kind of arch support in your running shoe. But you may have to lay off running for a while to let the plantar fascia heal.

Achilles Tendonitis

Achilles, according to legend, was vulnerable only in his heel, where, as an infant, his mother held him as she dipped him into the magical river Styx. Eventually, the warrior Paris hit Achilles in this spot with a poisoned arrow and killed him. For runners, Achilles tendonitis can be serious. The Achilles tendon is the thick band connecting the heel of the foot to the calf muscles, and when the sheath containing the tendon becomes inflamed, it tightens on the tendon, causing severe pain. The RICE technique can ease the pain, but rest is the only way to prevent further inflammation. If you try to run through the pain, you may end up tearing the tendon itself, which requires surgery and a long recovery period.

RUNNING **Tip**

When icing an injury, always place a thin layer of cloth, such as a washcloth, between the ice and your skin. Prolonged exposure to ice can harm your skin. Also, if you have bags of frozen peas or frozen corn in the freezer, use these instead of a bag of ice. Not only is this convenient, but since corn and peas are smaller than ice cubes, they enclose the injured area more effectively.

Stress Fractures

The most common form of stress fracture is to the metatarsals, which are the long, delicate bones, like spines of an umbrella, that run along the top of your foot to your toes. These can break under the strain of running long distances or pounding hard surfaces for prolonged times. An X-ray is necessary to determine whether you have in fact broken any of these bones, but if the top of your foot feels like a railroad spike has been jammed through it, a stress fracture is the likely cause. You're now looking at six weeks on the couch, with only ice and anti-inflammatories to help with the pain as you heal.

Runner's Knee

That cartilage around your kneecap that keeps your leg bending smoothly can't last forever. Eventually all those miles you cover are going to take their toll, and you'll find your knees throbbing with each step. When this happens, you need to give your knees a rest, cutting back on your miles or taking time off. Strengthening your thigh muscles—the quadriceps—helps, as does stabilizing your foot so that you don't overpronate (roll your foot in) or supinate (roll your foot out). But if you've done permanent damage to your cartilage, you may need surgical repair.

IT Band Injury

The IT, or iliotibial band, runs from your hip, down the outside of your thigh, to your knee. When this band tightens as a result of too much running, you feel a pain on the outside of your knee. This injury is a tough one to get rid of. There are IT band stretches that can help, but the best remedy is rest.

Runner's Butt

This injury is as unappealing as its name. Although I have never suffered this, a friend of mine has, and he describes it as a pain deep in his buttocks, right where the muscles on the back of his leg join up with the muscles in his rear end. This is where the piriformis muscle is located, and when this muscle becomes inflamed, running becomes very painful. The RICE treatment will not be very effective for pain relief because the muscle is too deep to reach in this way. Deep-tissue massage can offer relief, and there are various stretches that help, but like the other injuries, time off may be the most effective cure.

Dealing with Injury the Zen Way

Now, there might be a few runners who never encounter any of these injuries. However, the longer you run, the more likely it is that words like *iliotibial, fascia, tendonitis, metatarsal,* and *piriformis* will become part of your vocabulary. Although these words may impress your friends, to you they will mean only misery. But it doesn't have to be that way. No doubt, being happy is easier when you are healthy than when you are injured, but Zen can take the sting out of your time on the bench.

Suppose you've suffered an injury, and an involuntary vacation from running is now in your future. Let's first think about the emotions and thoughts that go through your head. Remember, you cannot overcome negative feelings until you identify them precisely.

Of course, each person reacts differently to serious injuries, based on the long-range diagnosis, the treatment plan, and so forth, but overall there are some fairly uniform emotional reactions to injury. Let's take a closer look at some of them.

Erasing Self-Pity

This one is *not* pretty. After I tore my gastrocnemius muscles, one of my first thoughts was *Why me?* What had I done to deserve such a cruel fate? What sins had I committed; what misdeeds had I performed? Why couldn't it have happened to someone else—my squash opponent, for instance? Without doubt, I was now the least fortunate person on Earth. Other runners with their other injuries had nothing on me. Me. ME. ME.

FROM THE MOUTHS *of Runners*

GREG 52, MICHIGAN "Injuries are horrible. It's amazing how quickly I can move from feeling like I'll run forever to feeling like I'll never run another step. I'm always afraid that after a week without running, I'll suddenly weigh 350 pounds and won't be able to walk to the refrigerator. Of course, once I get back to running, I realize I'm never in as bad shape as I thought I'd be."

Controlling Concerns about Loss of Conditioning

Unlike self-pity, this concern may be a valid source of anxiety. That doesn't mean you shouldn't try to control it, but it does mean there's less shame in taking it seriously. The prospect of spending two weeks on the road to recover the fitness you've lost from each week off the road is daunting. If your injury is serious, this may even take months. In my case, I essentially had to start from scratch.

Handling Withdrawal Pains

Runners, for the most part, enjoy running. A few people may muddle through only to lose weight or to gain other health benefits, but I'll go out on a limb and say that most runners *love* to run. They find relief from stress, take pride in goal achievement, and enjoy the simple pleasure that running affords them.

FROM THE MOUTHS *of Runners*

BILL 54, IOWA "A torn meniscus kept me out of serious running for a while until I had it repaired. The orthopedic surgeon advised me that my long-distance running days would be over—that was three Ironmans, two marathons, and four Syttende Mais ago! Can't keep an old runner down for long!"

Runners can become addicted to these feelings just as surely as drug addicts can become hooked on heroin. When an injury ends these pleasures, runners can feel despondent. A period of mournful withdrawal might follow.

I struggled through a period like this after my injury. I became quiet and moody. I no longer took as much pleasure in my family. My kids complained that I wouldn't play with them anymore. My wife complained that I was always grumpy. Life was not good.

Fortunately, this hard time did not last long. As soon as I began to apply my knowledge of Zen to the situation, matters improved quickly.

Choosing the Path to Zen Recovery

Zen can't help your body mend, but it can provide relief from the mental torments that runners experience while sidelined. The three kinds of torments we've looked at—self-pity, frustration at loss of conditioning, and sorrow that you can no longer enjoy running—are rooted in attachments of one kind or another. Attachments, you will recall, are the source of *dukkha*, or suffering. When you become attached to a particular idea, Buddhists believe, you are destined for trouble. This is because the world always changes, but attachments require that the world remains stable.

FROM THE MOUTHS *of Runners*

LYNN 38, WASHINGTON "Running is my mental health program. I get endorphins, time to be alone, time to chat with a friend. Because I wrecked my back with baby number three, I can only wog—walk-jog. Wogging doesn't give you the endorphins or nice muscle burn, but it's still an opportunity for fresh air and meditation."

Suppose, for instance, that you've attached yourself to the idea that dessert must always include chocolate. My wife has this attachment, and I do my best to accommodate it whenever I cook dessert. However, the world outside my kitchen is not always so friendly to my wife's needs. If we go to a restaurant where there is no chocolate on the dessert menu, or a dinner party where the host prepared a dessert *sans chocolat*, my wife is out of luck. Not only does she miss out on dessert (a tragedy on its own), but she also robs herself of opportunities to experience pleasures of a different kind: upside-down gingerbread pear cake, treacle tart, Grand Marnier soufflé, and so on. Because my wife cannot give up her attachment to the idea that dessert must contain chocolate, her future will not be as joyful as it could be.

Of course, missing out on some dessert is not quite the same as suffering (although some may think so). Attachments to other sorts of ideas, however, can be far more devastating. For this reason, Buddhists strive to live without attaching themselves to anything. In a world that is forever changing, any attachment, Buddhists believe, will inevitably lead to disappointment. For present purposes, the attachments that we need to think about are those that make injured runners miserable. Once we understand the exact nature of these attachments, they are fairly easy to give up.

Breaking the "I'm Special" Attachment

When injured runners look searchingly at the sky and ask "Why me?" they reveal an attachment to the idea that they are *special* in some sense. And if they are special, they don't *deserve* to be injured. "Why me?" is in fact a shorter way of asking "Why punish someone who is so clearly undeserving of an injury when there are so many others who are more deserving?" But, viewed this way, we can see that these runners' self-pity is out of place for a couple of reasons.

First, from the perspective of Zen, no person is more special than any other. The concept of humility is central to Buddhist ethics. No matter your achievements, you are no *better* than anyone else. Perhaps you are a successful doctor, lawyer, teacher, or police officer. Perhaps you care for children—your own or others'—or load vending machines or plow streets. All of these roles make particular contributions to human welfare. There are no grounds for judging people as better or worse on the basis of what they do.

Neither are some people superior because of the amount of money they possess, their physical attractiveness, or their age. In fact, the idea that your injury is unfair because it happened to you and not someone else is exactly wrong. Rather, the fact that it happened to you shows that it is an injury that really *could* happen to anyone. That, if anything, is evidence of fairness.

Another peculiarity of the "I'm Special" attachment is its assumption that your injury was "undeserved." This really is a strange assumption when you think about it. Injuries do not happen because they are *deserved.* You might say some runners "had it coming" if you know they pushed their body too hard, or ignored stretching exercises they were advised to do, but that is about *predicting* an injury, not *deserving* one. However, "Why me?" suggests the idea that there is some Divine Runner who dishes out injuries to naughty runners but spares good runners. And that is just silly.

BUDDHA **Says**

I do not believe in a fate that falls on people however they act. But I do believe in a fate that falls on them unless they act.

Zen rejects the idea that there is some divine plan about who will be injured and who will not. Injuries simply happen. An injury is one of countless events that take place in a world of constant change.

But there is more to self-pity than simply wondering "Why me?" Some runners believe that an injury affords them special treatment. For instance, when I indulged in self-pity after I tore my calf muscles, I convinced myself that I deserved special treatment for what I had suffered. Even if I wasn't special before the injury—no less "deserving" of an injury than anyone else—surely now that I had been injured I *was* special! My injury entitled me to be grumpy, to mope around the house in my slippers all day, to neglect responsibilities that I could easily meet.

This kind of self-pity exposes a different kind of attachment than the one we just considered. Apparently I had become attached to the idea that an injury endowed me with special privileges. Because I now had to walk with crutches, I *should* be excused for being grumpy; I should *not* be expected to help the children with their homework; I *deserved* a break from household chores that I could still perform without difficulty. This attachment to the idea that my injury had transformed me into royalty was, once recognized, simple to let go. While I could no longer be expected to perform duties that required two healthy legs, sustaining an injury did not make me special: I was no more worthy or valuable after an injury than I was before. I was simply *different*. I could no longer walk without the support of crutches, but—aside from a slightly different range of capabilities— this difference had no implications for how I should treat others or expect others to treat me.

BUDDHA **Says**

Those who are free of resentful thoughts surely find peace.

To summarize, when injured runners engage in self-pity, they betray attachments to ideas that are false. Injured runners are no more or less deserving of their lot than any other runners. All runners are, in the relevant sense, created equal. Thus, cries of "Why me?" have no basis. Moreover, injuries are not doled out by some

Divine Runner who has decided which runners deserve to be injured and which do not. Injuries happen. That's all there is to it. If one happens to you, you may be unlucky, but you are *not* being punished. Finally, being injured does not mean that you are now special and can expect to be pampered. Being injured is just another way of being. You no longer have capabilities that you used to have, but perhaps you do have capabilities that you didn't have before. Before you had to get up to close the door; now you can do it with a quick swipe of your crutch without having to leave your chair. Although attachment to these ideas can be strong, once you see them clearly and understand why they are false, it should be easier for you to fight off those ugly feelings of self-pity that afflict many injured runners.

Breaking the Attachment to the Idea of Permanence

A second negative emotion that troubles injured runners is anxiety about their loss of conditioning. This worry nagged me the most during my long unplanned hiatus from running. But why? What ideas had I become attached to that made a drop in physical fitness fill me with despair?

Here was one such thought: my efforts to acquire my former state of fitness had been for nothing. All that I had worked for! Gone without a trace. I had apparently become attached to the idea that fitness is only valuable if it can be maintained—that putting effort into something is not worthwhile unless its product can last forever.

Exposed in this light, the attachment is clearly misguided. Zen teaches that nothing lasts forever. People and things come and go.

Processes begin and end. The river that's now flowing past you is not the river that flowed past one minute ago, and it differs also from the river that will flow past a minute from now. Healthy people become sick, and sick people become healthy. The sun rises, moves across the sky, and sets. There is nothing in the world that is permanent. Only this moment, this *now*, exists, and just like that, it is gone and another *now* is in its place.

From this Zen perspective, an attachment to the idea that your efforts matter only if they can produce something permanent is guaranteed to cause you anguish. Because nothing is truly "forever," you must not begin a project or set yourself a goal whose success is measured by the creation of something permanent. If you do so, you are setting yourself up for heartbreak. You will have failed even before taking the first step.

BUDDHA **Says**

All things appear and disappear . . .

Appreciation of this point makes your loss of fitness less burdensome. Think about it: the effort you put into making yourself fit was not for nothing. How could it be? After all, the effort made you fit. That's an accomplishment of which to be proud. Yes—the loss of this fitness might seem unfortunate, but that does not undo all the hard work that's come before. It is unreasonable—irrational—to expect to remain fit all of your life. If this is the goal, why even bother trying? As a Zen runner, you must realize that as with everything, fitness and conditioning are merely temporary stages in your life.

Because fitness and conditioning are good things, they are worth working for, regardless of how long they may last. Injuries do not, despite appearances, undo the rewards of previous running. The reward was the fitness you had. To have hoped for more—for never-ending fitness—was to misunderstand the nature of the ever-changing world in which we live.

You may also become anxious about losing your fitness because you know how much hard work will be required to regain it. When I was finally healthy enough to run, my doctor told me that I shouldn't try to overdo things at first. My first runs should be no more than fifteen minutes. "Overdo it?" I thought. "Fifteen minutes?" On that first bright spring day, I set out at a pace slower than I had run for years, and I was sucking wind after only ten minutes. Someone had apparently wrapped my lungs in Ace bandages while I slept. My trip home was the longest mile I have ever walked. My head, hanging low, was full of thoughts about all the work I needed to do before I could enjoy once again my favorite 10K route. I was, I thought, right to have worried that I would have to begin all over again.

Well, I was right that I would have to begin all over again, but I *wasn't* right to have worried about it. I did not see that I had become attached to another false idea—the idea that hard work is bad. True, there was a lot of hard work in my future, but so what? I was, after all, running again. I now could experience the exhilaration of seeing myself slowly progress to my previous level of fitness. I'd done it before; I could do it again. Moreover, this time as I worked to achieve what I had lost, I could embrace a brand-new perspective on what running meant to me—a new appreciation for why I run and am fortunate to have running back in my life.

Breaking the Attachment to the Idea that Running Is the Only Key to Happiness

When people are deprived of something they enjoy immensely, it is no surprise that they feel sorrow. Most injured runners have to learn to deal with this sorrow of loss. After my injury, I regretted features of running that I hadn't even known I had enjoyed. Who would have thought I would miss waking up at 5 A.M., or that I liked feeling icicles forming on my eyelashes, or that icing my knees while watching the news was a great way to relax?

But lurking behind the pain of loss was an attachment that only made things worse. At some point in my history of running I became attached to the idea that I was a RUNNER. I was someone who could take pleasure in only one form of physical exercise: running. What RUNNERS do is run. They do not bicycle. They do not swim. Those endurance sports are for CYCLISTS and SWIMMERS. What of triathletes? As everyone knows, triathletes are not a natural kind of species. Really, they are either RUNNERS, CYCLISTS, or SWIMMERS who masquerade, from time to time, as other kinds of athletes. Triathletes are mutts of a sort, hybrids who have yet to recognize that they have no business mixing breeds.

In putting things this way, the folly of my attachment should be pretty clear. Although I could no longer be a RUNNER, I could be something else. Although I could no longer experience the joys of running, I could experience the joys of something else. Believe it or not, there is a reason that there are CYCLISTS and SWIMMERS in addition to RUNNERS. Cycling and swimming have their own pleasures to offer.

> **FROM THE MOUTHS** *of Runners*
>
> **KIT 39, OKLAHOMA** "My IT band injury sucks. But, on the other hand, it has forced me to expand my fitness horizons to . . . triathlons, yoga, kayaking . . . Sometimes I think I'm a better athlete *because* of my injury."

Although my injury prevented me from cycling, I could have spent my months away from running learning how to swim. When I began to train for the Ironman, I realized how foolish I had been to limit myself in that way. Suddenly I recognized that swimming has its own rhythm, brings its own kind of exhaustion, and provides opportunities for its own kind of meditative reflection. This is no less true of cycling.

My six months off the road would have gone much faster if I had realized that being a runner does not mean being a RUNNER—to the exclusion of other activities. Perhaps I would have discovered a new joy even greater than the one I find in running. Whatever the case, if (when!) you suffer an injury that prevents you from running, do not let yourself become attached to the idea that running is the only game in town. There are other games. Discover them.

Using Zen to Deal with Aging

While it's possible to run without ever suffering an injury, aging will catch up with all of us. Running can help keep you healthy and youthful, but it can't stop time. Case in point: I was about nineteen when I started to run. Now I'm older. This also happened to all my running acquaintances. If it hasn't yet happened to you, it will!

Here's another fact: as you get older, you slow down. At some point, you also have a harder time running those distances that you used to manage easily. This doesn't mean that you *are* slow or that you run only *short* distances. When I race, I am frequently passed by runners well into their sixties and perhaps older. But chances are high that they are slower than they were twenty years ago.

There's also no set recipe to dictate when you start to slow down. Some runners peak in their forties; others may peak in their fifties. I recently met a fifty-two-year-old woman who had just set her personal best in a 10K event. Nevertheless, I stand by my claim. Age catches up to all runners, and when it does, they face very different issues from those that trouble injured runners.

Here's the biggest difference. In most cases, injured runners can be very confident that in time they will overcome their injuries. They may not be able to run *now*, but they will recover and regain their previous distance and speed. In contrast, as you get older, there's no hope of becoming younger again. Life just doesn't work that way, and Zen can't change that. This means that as you age, you must approach your limitations differently. You can't "bounce back" from advanced age—a fact that many aging runners have a hard time accepting.

Getting to the Source of the Aging Runner's Concern

It can be harder to understand the dissatisfaction of aging runners than the concerns of injured runners. After all, the negative emotions that injured runners experience—self-pity, anxiety about fitness levels, and the sense of loss that comes when you can't do something enjoyable—are based on attachments to ideas that, for one reason or another, should be rejected.

But aging runners don't usually pity themselves—at least not for the reasons that injured runners do. The cry "Why me?" just doesn't make sense from the mouth of an aging runner. Injured runners struggle with the sense that their injury is unfair, because they compare themselves with others who have escaped a similar fate. But everyone grows older, so complaints about aging can't be about unfairness. In fact, compared to the alternative, growing old is something to celebrate!

FROM THE MOUTHS *of Runners*

DEAN 55, WISCONSIN "I don't worry too much about aging, but I get discouraged temporarily by injuries. So far, at least, I've been able to keep at it and overcome them, and I try to remember to be grateful for that. Eventually, I may have to pack it in, but meanwhile, even as I slow down, I'm still performing way beyond most people of all ages who don't put in the effort. Running has brought meaning to my life, and you can never take that away."

Also in contrast to injured runners, aging runners are unlikely to be concerned that all their work to date has been for naught. Runners do not lose their fitness as they age—not really. In fact, relative to their peers, a runner's fitness is probably even further above average when older than when younger. All that hard work has clearly *not* been for nothing. The older runners I know look and behave younger than their peers. Furthermore, they tell me that they have running to thank for their energy and health. They may not be as quick as they once were, but they feel just as fit and recognize the role that running has played in their well-being.

Finally, unlike injured runners, aging runners do not complain that they miss the joy of running, because they *do* run! Older runners are as able as any to enjoy moving through the world at a good clip, feeling the heat of the sun on their shoulders, watching the seasons change.

So, if self-pity, anxiety about fitness levels, and missed opportunities to run are not concerns for aging runners, why is aging a hard fact for many runners to accept? Why does the certainty that in future years we will no longer be able to maintain our current pace or run our longest distances bother so many runners? What, really, do runners who worry about aging have to worry about?

The answer, I think, is that aging runners measure themselves against their younger selves and take their present-day performance to be an indication that they are deteriorating. They are slower than they *used to be*. They lack the strength to run distances that they *could before*. The time it takes to recover after a race or a hard workout is longer now than it was *before*. In all these differences between now and then, the aging runner sees nothing but decline. Moreover, there's no good news on the horizon—no silver lining. If things are bad now, they're only going to get worse. This slide has no bottom.

Breaking the Attachment of the Aging Runner

Before we consider the attachment involved in the aging runners' fear of decline, let's recall the emphasis that Buddhists place on the idea that the world is constantly changing. The river is not the same as it was a moment ago or as it will be a moment from now. New water enters the river upstream. Old water spills from the river into the ocean. Soil erodes from some banks, and it accumulates in the delta. Everything in the world, Buddhists believe, is like this river. At every instant, the whole world is new—it contains things that didn't exist before and will never exist again.

This view of change—this denial of permanence—applies just as truly to people. People, are, after all, parts of the world. The person I was as a young child is not the person I am now. As a young child I didn't know things I now know; I believed things that I no longer believe. I weighed less than I do now. I was shorter. Likewise, the person I am now will not be the person who exists ten years or even ten minutes from now. The body's cells constantly die and get replaced with new cells. The thoughts I have now are not the thoughts I will have ten minutes from now.

ZEN **Practice**

Sit in front of a window and look out at the world. Notice details such as tree branches swaying in the wind, the length of shadows, and the positions of objects, including animals and people. Close your eyes for ten seconds and then look again. Is this the same world you see now?

You can see why this view is difficult to describe. In the Western view of the self, which I've just adopted here, I talk about myself when *I* was younger and myself when *I* will be older. But this way of talking is not consistent with Buddhism's view of change. The *I* who was younger is not the same *I* who is older. There is, Buddhists believe, no *I* who moves through time, because this would require that the *I* be something permanent—something that remains unchanged as the rest of the world changes around it.

Heavy, I know. But you don't have to completely understand or accept this Buddhist idea of the self to find something valuable within it. Consider again the negative emotion that runners experience as they age and find themselves slowing down. They see themselves as in decline, as deteriorating, as getting worse. They are not what they were *before*. They are not as good as they *used to be*.

BUDDHA **Says**

Every human being is the author of his own health
or disease.

Drawing on the Buddhist insight about change, we can see that this attitude shows an attachment to the idea that older runners are the same people they were as younger runners. Think about what the comparisons between your present performance and your past performance show about your conception of yourself. When you say that *you* are not as fast as *you* were before, you are comparing yourself now to yourself then. But Buddhists think this comparison is impossible. The you *now* is not the same person as the *you* who existed then, so there is no *you* who is getting slower, or deteriorating, or declining.

The Zen way to understand aging renders pointless the worries that runners typically express. This is because Zen denies that you are now the same person you were ten or twenty years ago. That person no longer exists. Moreover it was *that* person, not you, who was capable of running six-minute miles. Sure enough, that person was faster than you, but *your* abilities haven't deteriorated. Not at all. That's because *you* never could run that fast. That was someone else who did that. Someone you can admire. Someone you can be proud of. But not someone you should feel you are fighting a losing battle against.

Embracing the End of a Good Run

Thoughts of injury and aging strike terror in many runners' hearts. Injuries are painful and inconvenient. They prevent us from doing things we like to do. Aging forces us to slow down and to set our sights on different kinds of challenges than we might have tackled when younger.

I have found Zen to be a great comfort as I sit with ice on my knees, giving my body a week off to recover from aching cartilage. I also take solace in Zen as I notice that my body needs a bit more time every year to regain its strength after a race.

When someone asks me whether I ever plan to quit running, I answer no. I understand that as my body ages, I'll need to slow down. My body is not like Superman's. Doubtless there are injuries in my future and, unless I happen upon the fountain of youth (there are still parts of the local arboretum that I haven't explored!), getting older is a sure thing. If I take precautions—don't push myself, allow my injuries to heal, maintain a positive outlook—I should be okay. I should be able to run to my grave, so to speak. Right?

If only such guarantees were possible! At the core of Zen is the image of a constantly changing world, and, even though from my present vantage I see no obstacles in the way of running for the rest of my life, all that could change in an instant. A car accident could leave me disabled; a stroke could make it necessary for me to use a cane; a fall from my bike might ruin one of my knees. Any number of injuries can place a runner on the permanently disabled list. Similarly, not everyone will be lucky enough to age gracefully. The effects of aging on the body—and mind—are unpredictable, and although I know some codgers who still run thirty miles a week, I know other runners who, as they grow old, are simply unable to maintain a running schedule.

FROM THE MOUTHS *of Runners*

TESS 54, NEW JERSEY "I have had to learn to be more patient because I do get injured more easily and don't recover as quickly as I used to. This means, for example, that I never run two days in a row. That's okay with me, though, as I enjoy lots of different activities."

In short, many runners fear injury and aging because they worry about what these events forebode. The plain fact is that for some unfortunate runners, the future will not cooperate. They will no longer be able to run ever again. We can all hope that we never see this time, but some of us will. That's just how life is.

But how can you prepare for such an event? Lots of runners cannot imagine life without running. I'm like that. Running is a fixture in my life. Even so, despite all that running means to me, I don't think that life must end if and when I must cease to run. If a time comes when I am no longer able to run, life will be *different*, but it will not be *worse*.

Looked at the Zen way, there are two lives to consider here. There is the life of the runner—the life before the injury or aging put a stop to running—and the life after. The runner's life is in the past. Your life is in the present. Pining for the past life can bring nothing but *dukkha*, or suffering, to the present life. You must let go of the runner's life and embrace the life you have now. You must live *who you are* in *this* moment.

I think this perspective is potentially very soothing. Don't ask yourself to do something beyond your present ability; ask yourself what you need to do *now* to live a happy and fulfilled life. Now you are not a runner. That person is gone. Instead, you are a person with talents, skills, hobbies, interests, and goals—and that's what you should be pursuing.

BUDDHA **Says**
He is able who thinks he is able.

Remember the Ugly Duckling? It so desperately wanted to be something it wasn't—something it could never be. But the misery was pointless, as misery always is when it is directed toward something that cannot be changed. A swan cannot be a duck, but it is beautiful in its own right—more beautiful, even, than a duck. Once you can no longer run, you're no longer a runner, and feeling miserable is equally pointless. You are now someone else, and this is the person you should care about. This is the person who will grow into a swan.

If you do become a person who cannot run, think of yourself as embarking on a new life. This is no metaphor. Your life is new. It is no longer the life of someone who gets up early to run, or who trains for races, or who meets friends for a leisurely 10K. You are now someone who has more time for exploring new challenges. Perhaps you can perfect that swimming stroke that has eluded you for so long. Maybe a cruise vacation is in order, the sort that would never occur to someone who needs to run 5K every day. Perhaps you might start writing that book that's always been on the back of your mind. Your life now contains time for any or all of these activities. Seize this new life, and feel happy to have known that runner you used to be.

CHAPTER 8
FOLLOWING A PEACEFUL PATH

In the seventeenth century, the great Dutch scientist Christiaan Huygens discovered something quite surprising. He had suspended two pendulum clocks from a wooden beam and found that after a time, the motion of the pendulums in the clocks became synchronized—they began and ended their swings at exactly the same time. If he stopped one pendulum and then started it again, after a while its movements would again become synchronized with the movements of the other pendulum. It was as if some magical force guided the motions of the pendulums so they would stay in step with each other.

Of course, the explanation of this strange phenomenon doesn't really involve magic. On careful examination, Huygens noticed that the motions of the pendulums were causing very slight wobbles in the beam that supported them, and these barely perceptible vibrations were responsible for the synchronization. Huygens's discovery has stuck with me because it is a perfect example of how two separate activities can be brought into harmony with each other without any special effort. Neither pendulum is *trying* to make the other behave like *it* is behaving. It just *happens* that the motions of the two pendulums will end up precisely coordinated with each other. The influence each pendulum has on the other is automatic and effortless, but the resulting harmony between the two makes it seem *as if* someone must have started the pendulums swinging at the same moment.

I think Huygens's discovery provides a wonderful metaphor for how the Zen lessons you incorporate into your running can automatically and effortlessly influence how you live. There's no reason the Zen attitudes that contribute to successful running can't *also* contribute to successful living. This final chapter is about using running to bring harmony to your life.

Zen in Your Life

When you think about it, the idea that running might teach you something about life shouldn't be too shocking. In a fairly obvious sense, running is life made small. A run has a beginning and an end. There are obstacles to overcome, good days and bad days. You pass some people and get passed by others. There are tests and challenges, disappointments and achievements, days you feel you have nothing left to give and other days when you feel you can go forever. Because there are so many parallels between running and living, the Zen tools that enhance and facilitate your running can do the same for your quality of life.

Life, as we all know, is very complicated. As a graduate student, I tried to learn a kind of logic known as *recursion theory*. This is hard stuff, and I didn't get too far with it. My professor, a very kind man, was one of the smartest people I have ever met. When I told him that recursion theory was just too complicated for me, he replied, "But recursion theory is simple compared to life! Life is far more complicated."

Personally, I seem to have an easier time living than I do solving proofs in recursion theory. However, his comment expresses an important insight: life *is* complicated. At any instant there may be five or six pressing demands on our time, the future is not always easy to predict, well-conceived plans go awry. Consequently, it is easier to learn Zen principles in the relatively uncomplicated context of running than it is in the vast and complex domain of life. Running is a great place to cut your Zen teeth. Then you'll be better prepared to apply it to something really hard, like life.

Let's suppose that you've experimented with Zen while running, training, racing, and recovering. If so, you should have a pretty good sense of how to make Zen work for you. The practices of mindfulness, right effort, and meditation should feel familiar. You should always be looking for The Middle Way. The idea of impermanence should no longer be quite so hard to fathom. If you've reached this point in your Zen training, the time has come to begin applying your newfound wisdom to problems that you face outside the running arena. As you encounter life's difficulties, you simply translate them into running difficulties, which you are now well prepared to handle. Some examples will illustrate how to do this.

Viewing Work as That Same Old Path

Many people think of work as an unpleasant task that occupies the time between breakfast and dinner. It's the same old thing, day after day. There are many activities they would rather be doing if given the chance. If you have this attitude toward work, you should consider how your Zen training helps you through those long runs when there's nothing of particular note to hold your attention. Or, you might view work as a running path that you've done over and over again. When you translate your working blues into the vocabulary of a runner, you are ready to think about them in the Zen terms you have learned.

You might start with mindfulness and right effort. If you were bored with your running route, you would ask yourself why you feel that way. Here, ask yourself why you are bored with your job. What attachments are causing your dissatisfaction? Perhaps you are attached to the idea that every day must be new and exciting, or that you deserve better, or that you have better things to do with your time. Reflect hard on these ideas. Why must every day hold new experiences? Why do you deserve better? What would you be doing all day long if you were not working?

Zen methods can also help you through the tedium of the workday. Instead of focusing on the similarities in your daily work routine, concentrate on the differences. What's changed in the office around you? What makes today's tasks not quite like yesterday's or tomorrow's? I bet it is simply not true that every day at work is just like every other day. Challenge yourself to find the differences. At the same time, take pleasure in the familiar. Don't slump into your office chair every morning and put yourself on autopilot. Instead, take some time to *notice* your surroundings. Be aware of the texture of your chair's upholstery, the firmness of its cushion. Look at the wood grain on your desktop. Survey the world outside your window. This is your chair, your desk, your view. Think of these things as reliable old friends who are present to greet you every morning.

Seeing Relationships as Training Runs

All relationships—whether with parents, children, friends, spouses, partners, or coworkers—are a source of occasional anxiety. Maintaining a relationship takes work. Hard work. You're often called on to do or say or accept things that you'd rather not. Why bother? Because you know that whatever the current hardship you are weathering, your relationship is valuable to you. The other person is an important part of your life.

ZEN **Practice**

Think about sources of anxiety or unhappiness in your life. To what aspects of running can you compare them? Are they steep hills, icy conditions, injuries, disappointing results? Once you fix on a suitable comparison, try to apply the Zen tools that you've used to deal with the running problem to deal with your life problem.

In many respects, relationships are like training runs. There are steep hills you must climb, sprints that leave you exhausted, and periods when you are not sure whether the struggle is worth it. Viewed this way, you can put your training experiences to good use when you encounter relationship difficulties. The Zen techniques that help with training can also help you overcome tough times in your relationships.

When you think of relationships as training runs, it is natural to look for The Middle Way that promises to smooth over whatever rough patches are currently harming them. We saw that training is ineffective if you don't push yourself enough, but dangerous if you push yourself too much. This is just as true in relationships. Sometimes strife in a relationship is the product of differences in expectations. You might expect too much from your spouse or child or friend. If this is the complaint, re-evaluate your expectations. Try setting them lower and see whether the situation improves. If your spouse complains that it's too difficult to meet the kids after school every day, place a hot meal on the table every evening, or tolerate your constant travels, lower these expectations for a trial period. You might find that your spouse is happier, which makes your life, despite the changes, happier too. If the changes don't work, seek another Middle Way. Unless your spouse's expectations are hopelessly out of balance with your own, there's a Middle Way out there. You just have to find it.

Similarly, antagonisms with coworkers or employers often result because you have not found the appropriate Middle Way. If you feel that your coworkers are taking advantage of you, or that your boss is exploiting you, you need to speak up. This kind of confrontation is very hard for most people. Think of it as a steep hill that you must climb, or as a speed interval you must run. You know how to prepare yourself for these tests, and the same techniques can work in this situation. Perhaps you'll want to meditate first in order to clear your mind and relax yourself. Don't think of your coworkers as competitors in a race—as people you hope to defeat. Look on them as a means to challenge yourself. Your goal is to make them understand your perspective. They are hills to be climbed, not flattened. Make a case for The Middle Way as you see it. What strikes you as a fair distribution of labor? How might you work together more successfully? Of course, if your coworkers are simply unreasonable, there may not be much hope in convincing them of the appropriate Middle Way, but you'll probably be no worse off for having tried.

Treating Hardships as Injuries

In the previous chapter, I described several Zen methods for dealing with injuries. Injuries are painful not just because they hurt, but because they prevent us from doing what we like to do. They make us worry that the effort we have put into conditioning ourselves is going to waste. They remind us of our mortality and of the possibility that some day we may no longer be able to run.

Injuries and their consequences have counterparts in everyday life. You might score poorly on an LSAT exam, all but ending your chance to attend the law school of your dreams. A loved one might die, creating a terrible absence in your life. An accident or illness might prevent you from enjoying future travel plans, or might force you to make significant changes to your lifestyle. In short, bad things happen, and when they do, you must live with their consequences. But, although bad things are never welcome, the same Zen practices that can help you through injuries can also help you through the hardships that are a part of life.

Mindfulness can take the sting out of some hardships. If you can't enter the law school of your dreams, you should try to uncover the attachments that made *that* law school seem like the only option. Injured runners may feel heartbroken to learn that they will never be able to regain their previous top speed. But why is this goal the only possibility for happiness? Similarly, why is this law school the only one worth attending?

FROM THE MOUTHS *of Runners*

HANNAH 51, FLORIDA "I think of myself as a runner. I enjoy other sports . . . tennis, golf, cycling, softball . . . but those are more for fun. I think about running as part of who I am. There are ups and downs, good runs and not-so-good runs . . . but it doesn't matter because like each day, each run will bring something new."

Right effort, you will discover, is a useful tool for dealing with most hardships. Remember that you are in charge of how you react to bad news or undesirable outcomes. A divorce, for instance, is no doubt a painful event. But it's up to you whether to let a divorce make you bitter and prevent you from forming new relationships. Once divorced, put the pain behind you. When you think back on your marriage, focus on the happy moments it contained rather than the tormented ones. Instead of seeing the marriage as an investment gone bad, think of it as an experience that will make you a better spouse or partner in the future. Look on your new status as a single person as an opportunity to feel once more the excitement and highs that come with falling in love again.

The Zen idea of impermanence—which can help a runner accept the impossibility of ever recovering fully from an injury, or ever again achieving accomplishments that were once within easy reach, or, worst of all, ever running again at all—can also be of great comfort when facing potentially life-changing events. We have seen that much of the *dukkha*, or suffering, that runners feel when they are no longer capable of past feats is the consequence of a misperception about the nature of reality. If you think that you are the same person now that you were ten years ago, or before that injury, or before gaining weight, then you might think of *your* new pace as slower than *your* old pace; you might conclude that the distances *you* now run are shorter than the distances *you* used to run. Furthermore, you might take these as signs that *you* are a worse runner than *you* used to be. But, once you understand that nothing is permanent, that every second brings with it a new world, the idea that you are worse than you used to be is no longer coherent. There was an individual *then*, and there is another—different—individual *now*. The individual *then* may have run a seven-minute mile, and the individual *now* may run a nine-minute mile. But this doesn't reveal a worsening, because there is no single individual whose performance declined over time. There are two individuals who happen to be able to run at different speeds.

The perspective of impermanence, I believe, makes the acceptance of life-changing events much easier. Suppose you lose a lot of money in the stock market, or you are laid off from your job, or your marriage ends, or a car accident forces you into a wheelchair. It is tempting to see some of these events as failures, or as marking a significant deterioration in the quality of your life. But to see something as a failure or as a cause of deterioration is to assume that you are the same person you used to be, but now your situation is worse than it was before. You don't have it as good as you used to. But try now to apply the idea of impermanence. You haven't lost anything, because you are not the person who existed before. It was someone else with a lot of money in stocks, or with a job, or a spouse, or two healthy legs. Think about people you now know who have more money than you. You bear the same relation to this person as you do to that former self who had substantial resources in the stock market. But, you are not a failure because you don't have as much money as that person. You certainly have not *lost* anything because that person has more money than you do. Once you understand this point, events that on an ordinary way of thinking seem to lessen your life can be seen instead to *create* life. Changes are not "for the worse." Rather, changes create new lives that must accept new challenges and set new goals. That's not bad. That's just how it is.

Celebrating a Runner's Life

Running is for me a special activity. It brings value to my life while at the same time it teaches me how to value life.

Zen has played a significant role in the evolution of my perspective on running. Though I don't regard myself as a spiritual person, at least in the usual sense of this term, I have come to regard running as something holy. Running makes me a better person. Running, for me, is transformative. I have learned self-discipline and patience from running. I have also learned how to compete with grace, and how to face hardships with optimism. I hope the lessons conveyed in this book do the same for you, or at least encourage you to search for the same fulfillment through running.

APPENDIX
BUDDHISM RESOURCES

BOOKS ABOUT BUDDHISM

The growing popularity of Buddhism in the West has spawned a number of good and accessible beginner's guides to Buddhism. Still, I have found no author clearer or more inspirational than His Holiness the Dalai Lama. Among my favorite books of his are:

The World of Tibetan Buddhism: An Overview of Its Philosophy and Practice, Wisdom Publications, 1995.

How to Practice: The Way to a Meaningful Life, Atria Publications, 2001.

An Open Heart: Practicing Compassion in Everyday Life, Little, Brown and Company, 2001.

Other books that offer useful discussions of Buddhist history, philosophy, and practice include these:

The Heart of the Buddha's Teaching, by Thich Nhat Hanh, Broadway, 1999.

Buddhism for Beginners, by Thubten Chodron, Snow Lion Publications, 2001.

Zen and the Art of Happiness, by Chris Prentiss, Power Press, 2006.

BUDDHISM INTERNET RESOURCES

The Internet has become a useful resource for learning about Buddhism generally and Zen Buddhism more specifically. Although there are many valuable sites, I have found these particularly enlightening:

www.zenguide.com
www.thezensite.com
www.thebigview.com/buddhism

OTHER ZEN INTERNET RESOURCES

In addition to the Buddhism guides, some websites offer material that can be instructional (and fun!) to look at:

www.ashidakim.com/zenkoans/zenindex.html

This site contains a collection of Zen koans, which are short parables or riddles that Zen monks contemplate in order to "shock" themselves into states of enlightenment. A Zen teacher might also present koans to disciples as a way to test their understanding of Zen.

www.brainyquote.com/quotes/authors/b/buddha.html

This site contains a list of quotations from the Bhudda, including the quotations that appeared in this book.

www.google.com/ Top/Society/Religion_and_Spirituality /Buddhism/Lineages/Zen/Centers

If you'd like to find Zen practitioners near you, you should visit a local Zen center. This site lists Zen centers throughout the world.

ABOUT THE AUTHOR

Larry Shapiro, PhD, grew up in New Jersey and Philadelphia, and now lives in Madison, Wisconsin, where he is a full professor in the Department of Philosophy at the University of Wisconsin. He has run a number of marathons and half marathons, and has a drawer full of T-shirts from various 10k events. In 2006 he competed in Madison's Ironman tournament. He'll run between twenty and thirty miles per week when not training, and between thirty and forty when preparing for a race. Shapiro has published widely in philosophy, and his international reputation provides him with opportunities to run in locations around the world. But still his favorite place to run is in an arboretum a few blocks from his house in Madison, where he lives with his wife, Athena, and daughters Thalia and Sophia.